TTT速習シリーズ

TOEIC® L&Rテスト
Part 5
語彙問題だけ555

はじめに

　TOEIC® L&Rテスト（以下TOEIC）Part 5のほぼ半分を占めているのが、空所に当てはまる適切な意味の語句を選ぶ問題（語彙問題）です。

　文法で解くタイプの問題は文法のルールを身につければカバーできますが、語彙問題は対策しにくいと感じている人が多いのではないでしょうか。単語を一つひとつ覚えないと解けないし、問題を解いても正解しか記憶に残らず、誤答の選択肢は意味も使い方も確認しないままで終わってしまう……思い当たる方も多いことでしょう。

　これは実にもったいないことです。その問題では誤答でも、他の問題で正解になることがありますし、別のパート、たとえばPart 7の文書で使われていて、その語句が分からないと正解を選べないことも十分にあり得るからです。誤答だからという理由で選択肢の4分の3を捨ててしまうなんて、繰り返しになりますが、本当にもったいないことです。

　「誤答選択肢も復習しましょう」と言うのは簡単ですが、誤答ですから、文の中での使われ方は問題文から読み取れません。語彙を覚えるなら、文の中でその語句がどのように使われるかもセットで知っておく必要があります。

　本書は、こうした問題意識から生まれた、Part 5の語彙問題を集中的にトレーニングするための本です。以下の特長を備えています。

1. 語彙問題だけ555問徹底演習

　555問のPart 5語彙問題をコンパクトな1冊にギュッとまとめました。これ1冊で、TOEIC約40回分の語彙問題に取り組むことができます。

2. 1セットの選択肢を4問でシェア

　本書の大きな特長がこれです。4つの選択肢のうち、ある問題では(A)が正解でも、他の問題では(B)が正解になることがあり得ます。そこで、4つの選択肢に対してそれぞれが正解になるような英文を作成して4つの問題にしています。同じ選択肢のセットを4回吟味して解答し、それぞれが正解にな

る文を読むことで、4つの選択肢すべてを吸収することができます。捨てる選択肢はありません。

3. 公式問題から厳選した選択肢

選択肢として使用した語彙は、日本と韓国で発売されているETS公式問題の英文素材で使われた語彙から厳選しています。Part 5頻出語にはとらわれずに選びました。Part 7の文書で使われた語彙が、数カ月後にはPart 5の選択肢に出現してもおかしくないのがTOEICですから、Part 5頻出語だけでなく他のパートに出てきた語も重要、と考えてのことです。

4. 「もう1問！」ですぐに復習

4問のうち1問は、別の語句を空所にした問題を掲載しています。捨てるところがないのは選択肢だけではありません。Part 5の英文で使われる語句はいつ出題されてもおかしくありませんから、問題文の隅々まで復習することが、手間なようで結局はスコアアップの近道になります。「もう1問！」を復習に役立ててください。

5. リアルな問題文

出題されるトピック、文の長さなど「TOEICらしさ」を意識して作成・チューニングしました。

6. 強力な執筆陣

アルクの「TOEIC® L&Rテストスコアアップ指導者養成講座」(TTT) を修了した、TOEIC指導の最前線で活躍する講師陣が、訳と解説の執筆を担当しました。TOEICについての深い知識と経験、指導力が随所に盛り込まれた、コンパクトながら充実した解説になっています。

本書を隅々まで楽しんで味わっていただけること、そして、目標スコア達成のお役に立てることを願っています。

2020年4月
西嶋愉一
勝山庸子、小林佳奈子、下窄称美、山田 治

TOEIC® L&Rテスト
Part 5
語彙問題だけ555！

CONTENTS

本書の構成と使い方

本書は、Part 5「短文穴埋め問題」の中でも、選択肢に同じ品詞の語が並ぶ「語彙問題」だけを集めた問題集です。選択肢のセットは4問につき1つ。1問解くたびに選択肢を吟味するので、各語句の意味や用法をより深く考えることになります。また、4問中1問は別の重要語句を空所にして再出題。1課で5つの重要語句がしっかり身に付きます。

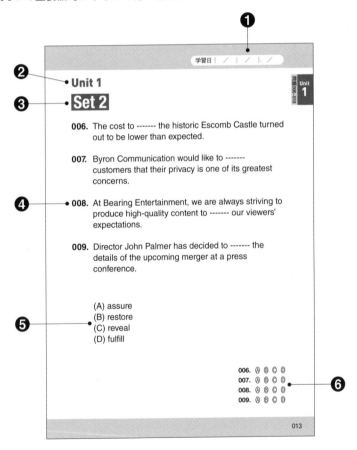

❶

学習日 ｜ ／ ｜ ／ ｜ ／

❷ Unit 1

❸ Set 2

問題 006-010 Unit 1

006. The cost to ------- the historic Escomb Castle turned out to be lower than expected.

007. Byron Communication would like to ------- customers that their privacy is one of its greatest concerns.

❹ **008.** At Bearing Entertainment, we are always striving to produce high-quality content to ------- our viewers' expectations.

009. Director John Palmer has decided to ------- the details of the upcoming merger at a press conference.

❺
(A) assure
(B) restore
(C) reveal
(D) fulfill

❻
006. (A) (B) (C) (D)
007. (A) (B) (C) (D)
008. (A) (B) (C) (D)
009. (A) (B) (C) (D)

013

❶ 学習日記入欄 ── 時間をおいて2度復習すると効果的。
❷ ユニット番号 ── 計10ユニット(Unit 1～10)。
❸ セット番号 ── 各ユニットにつき11セット(Set 1～11)。Unit 10のみ12セット。
❹ 問題 ── 4問。
❺ 選択肢 ── 4問共通。
❻ 解答欄 ── 復習時のために鉛筆など消せる筆記具で塗ろう。
❼ 品詞 ── どの品詞の問題かを示す。
❽ 全選択肢の訳
❾ 各問題の正解記号と問題文の訳
❿ 解説 ── 4問共通。
⓫「もう1問!」── 4問中1問の別の語句を空所にした問題。

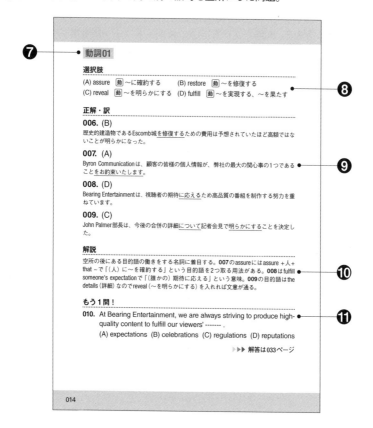

❼ 動詞01

選択肢

(A) assure [動]〜に確約する　　(B) restore [動]〜を修復する
(C) reveal [動]〜を明らかにする　(D) fulfill [動]〜を実現する、〜を果たす ── ❽

正解・訳

006. (B)
歴史的建造物であるEscomb城を修復するための費用は予想されていたほど高額ではないことが明らかになった。

007. (A)
Byron Communicationは、顧客の皆様の個人情報が、弊社の最大の関心事の1つであることをお約束いたします。 ── ❾

008. (D)
Bearing Entertainmentは、視聴者の期待に応えるため高品質の番組を制作する努力を重ねています。

009. (C)
John Palmer部長は、今後の合併の詳細について記者会見で明らかにすることを決定した。

解説
空所の後にある目的語の働きをする名詞に着目する。**007**のassureにはassure + 人 + that 〜で「(人)に〜を確約する」という目的語を2つ取る用法がある。**008**はfulfill someone's expectationで「(誰かの)期待に応える」という意味。**009**の目的語はthe details(詳細)なのでreveal(〜を明らかにする)を入れれば文意が通る。 ── ❿

もう1問!

010. At Bearing Entertainment, we are always striving to produce high-quality content to fulfill our viewers' ------- . ── ⓫
　　　(A) expectations　(B) celebrations　(C) regulations　(D) reputations

▶▶▶ 解答は033ページ

本書の音声について

本書対応の音声教材として、空所に正解語句を補った問題文（444文）と、その訳文の読み上げ音声を無料提供しています。問題文を繰り返し聞くことで、正しい文の形や、コロケーション（よくある語句の組み合わせ）に耳がなじみ、本番のテストで時間をかけずに解答できる問題が増えます。ぜひ、活用してください。

音声はMP3形式で、アルクのダウンロードセンターからパソコンにダウンロードする方法と、専用アプリを用いてスマートフォンに直接ダウンロードする方法があります。詳しくは右ページをご覧ください。

フォルダ構成と音声データファイル名

音声データは2種類のフォルダ（アルバム）に分かれています。

● **問題文のみの音声データフォルダ：7020022_E**
　ファイル名の例　001_E.mp3（例文番号001の問題文音声データ）

● **問題文と訳文の音声データフォルダ：7020022_EJ**
　ファイル名の例　001_EJ.mp3（例文番号001の問題文・訳文音声データ）

音声ダウンロードのご案内

本書の音声教材は、パソコン、もしくはスマートフォンにダウンロードしてご利用ください。ダウンロードにはインターネット接続が必要です。なお、ファイルサイズが大きいため、ダウンロードに時間がかかり、通信料がかさむ場合があります。ブロードバンド環境（Wi-Fi環境）でのご利用をお勧めします。

パソコンにダウンロードする場合

パソコンへの音声ファイルのダウンロードは、下記のURLから行ってください。

アルクのダウンロードセンター
https://www.alc.co.jp/dl/

※書名もしくは商品コード（7020022）で検索してください。
※ダウンロード後、zipファイルを解凍してご利用ください。パソコンのOSによっては、圧縮ファイルの解凍ソフト（Lhaplusなど）が必要な場合があります。

スマートフォンにダウンロードする場合

スマートフォンに直接ダウンロードするには、専用アプリのインストールが必要です。下記の2つの選択肢があります。

語学のオトモALCO【無料】

アルクが提供する語学学習用のアプリで、Android、iOSに対応しています。再生スピードの変更や数秒単位の巻き戻し・早送り、2点間リピートなどの機能を備えています。

abceed analytics【無料】

株式会社Globeeが提供する語学学習用アプリで、Android、iOSに対応しています。自動採点・分析機能を備え、マークシートで解答・採点できます。

ご利用の際は、下記のURLからスマートフォンにアプリをダウンロードしてください。

https://www.
globeejapan.
com/

abceed analyticsにおける本書のサービス内容は、予告なく変更になる場合があります。

「語学のオトモ ALCO」をご活用ください

「語学のオトモ ALCO」アプリは、書籍・通信講座の音声、通信講座の電子版テキストブックをダウンロードして利用する専用アプリです。

ALCOでできること

● 本書の音声をスマホで聞ける！

CD-ROMドライブ付きパソコンがなくても大丈夫。スマートフォンにALCOをインストールすれば、本書の音声をスマートフォンに直接ダウンロードし、聞くことができきます。

● 再生スピードを調節できる！

再生スピードを0.5倍〜3倍まで調節できる話速変換機能を備えています。本書の問題音声が速すぎると感じる場合は、スライダーを動かしてスピードを遅くしてみましょう。

● 聞きたいところだけリピート再生できる！

音声でA地点、B地点を指定して、AB2区間の音声を再生できます。何度も繰り返し聞けるので、ディクテーションやリピーティングの練習に便利です。

● 巻き戻し・早送りが便利！

再生中にボタンを押すだけで、指定した秒数（2、4、8、16、30秒）での巻き戻しや早送りができます。聞きたいところをピタリと指定できるのでストレスがありません。

ご注意

※1 「語学のオトモ ALCO」はApp Store（iPhone）、Google Play（アンドロイド）からダウンロードできます。ご利用にはメールアドレスIDの登録が必要です。詳細は　https://www.alc.co.jp/alco/　をご覧ください。

※2 ご利用条件（https://www.alc.co.jp/policy/other/）を必ずご確認のうえ、同意いただける方のみご利用ください。

※3 ダウンロードコンテンツには容量の大きいものが多いため、ダウンロードの際はWi-Fi環境でのご利用を推奨いたします。また、スマートフォンの内蔵メモリにファイルサイズ相当の空き容量が必要です。

※4 本サービスの内容は予告なく変更する場合があります。あらかじめご了承ください。

Unit 1
Set 1

001. There is an additional charge when passengers bring oversized ------- on Stuart Air's discount flights.

002. The Annual Lincoln Music Festival will host hundreds of musicians from a wide range of ------- .

003. Bancshares Construction requested three ------- of building materials in order to verify their quality.

004. Mori Motors' sales ------- show that there is strong demand for their new electric car models.

(A) genres
(B) items
(C) samples
(D) figures

名詞01

選択肢

(A) genres 名 ジャンル　　　　　(B) items 名 物、品目、商品
(C) samples 名 サンプル　　　　　(D) figures 名 数字、形

正解・訳

001. (B)
Stuart Airの格安便に（規定より）大きな物を持ち込む乗客には追加料金が課される。
oversized: 大き過ぎる　charge: 料金、手数料

002. (A)
毎年恒例のLincoln 音楽祭は、さまざまなジャンルのミュージシャンを招いて開催される。
host: ～を主催する

003. (C)
Bancshares Constructionは、品質を検証するために建築材料のサンプルを3つ要求した。
verify: ～を検証する

004. (D)
Mori Motorsの販売数は、新型の電気自動車のモデルに強い需要があることを示している。

解説

001のitemには「物、項目、商品」の意味があるが、ここでは「物」＝「荷物」を指している。**003**のように、TOEICでは品質を確かめるためにサンプルを要求する、という状況がしばしば登場する。**004**のsales figuresは「売上高、販売数量」を指すTOEIC頻出表現だ。ちなみに、figureには「形、図」という意味もある。

もう1問！

005. There is an additional charge when passengers bring ------- items
on Stuart Air's discount flights.

(A) exaggerated　(B) widespread　(C) oversized　(D) customized

▶▶▶ 解答は033ページ

Unit 1

Set 2

006. The cost to ------- the historic Escomb Castle turned out to be lower than expected.

007. Byron Communication would like to ------- customers that their privacy is one of its greatest concerns.

008. At Bearing Entertainment, we are always striving to produce high-quality content to ------- our viewers' expectations.

009. Director John Palmer has decided to ------- the details of the upcoming merger at a press conference.

(A) assure
(B) restore
(C) reveal
(D) fulfill

006. Ⓐ Ⓑ Ⓒ Ⓓ
007. Ⓐ Ⓑ Ⓒ Ⓓ
008. Ⓐ Ⓑ Ⓒ Ⓓ
009. Ⓐ Ⓑ Ⓒ Ⓓ

選択肢

(A) assure 動 ～に確約する   (B) restore 動 ～を修復する

(C) reveal 動 ～を明らかにする   (D) fulfill 動 ～を実現する、～を果たす

正解・訳

006. (B)

歴史的建造物であるEscomb城を修復するための費用は予想されていたほど高額ではないことが明らかになった。

007. (A)

Byron Communicationは、顧客の皆様の個人情報が、弊社の最大の関心事の1つであることをお約束いたします。

008. (D)

Bearing Entertainmentは、視聴者の期待に応えるため高品質の番組を制作する努力を重ねています。

009. (C)

John Palmer部長は、今後の合併の詳細について記者会見で明らかにすることを決定した。

解説

空所の後にある目的語の働きをする名詞に着目する。**007**のassureにはassure＋人＋that～で「(人)に～を確約する」という目的語を2つ取る用法がある。**008**は fulfill someone's expectationで「(誰かの)期待に応える」という意味。**009**の目的語はthe details(詳細)なのでreveal(～を明らかにする)を入れれば文意が通る。

もう1問！

010. At Bearing Entertainment, we are always striving to produce high-quality content to fulfill our viewers' ------- .

     (A) expectations   (B) celebrations   (C) regulations   (D) reputations

▶▶▶ 解答は033ページ

Unit 1
Set 3

011. As a result of his reputation for fairness and dependability, Stephen Dalton is highly ------- among fellow Baltimore businesspeople.

012. The Summer Breeze Spa provides ------- treatments to suit your individual needs.

013. The highly ------- mechanics at DTT Automotive can repair most makes and models in a few hours.

014. At the annual meeting, shareholders discussed a ------- merger with a rival company.

(A) respected
(B) skilled
(C) personalized
(D) proposed

011. Ⓐ Ⓑ Ⓒ Ⓓ
012. Ⓐ Ⓑ Ⓒ Ⓓ
013. Ⓐ Ⓑ Ⓒ Ⓓ
014. Ⓐ Ⓑ Ⓒ Ⓓ

形容詞01

選択肢

(A) respected 動形 尊敬されている　(B) skilled 形 熟練した、腕の良い
(C) personalized 動形 個人の好みに合わせた
(D) proposed 動形 提案された

正解・訳

011. (A)

公平で信頼できるという評判の結果として、Stephen Dalton は Baltimore の経営者仲間から非常に<u>尊敬されている</u>。

012. (C)

The Summer Breeze Spa は、あなた個人の要求を満たすため、<u>個人の好みに合わせた</u>施術を提供している。

013. (B)

非常に<u>熟練した</u> DTT Automotive の整備士は、たいていのメーカーやモデルの車を数時間で修理することができる。
make:（自動車の）メーカー／model: 車種

014. (D)

年次総会で、株主らは<u>提案された</u>ライバル会社との合併について議論した。

解説

語尾に ed が付く動詞の過去分詞もしくは形容詞が並んでいる。**012** は、personalized（個人の好みに合わせた）を選ぶと、文の後半の「あなた個人の要求を満たす」という文脈に合う。**013** の mechanic（整備士）を修飾する語として適切なのは (B) の skilled（熟練した）だ。**014** は proposed merger（提案された合併）とすると文意が通る。

もう1問！

015. The Summer Breeze Spa provides personalized treatments to ------- your individual needs.

　　　(A) react (B) suit (C) cater (D) take

▶▶▶ 解答は033ページ

Unit 1
Set 4

016. Please make sure that all of the equipment in the conference room is working ------- before the guests arrive.

017. Our sales representatives are trained to answer ------- asked questions from customers.

018. Corecoms Industries Inc. is looking for ------- motivated engineers to join our research and development team.

019. Over the last few years, shopping for office supplies online has ------- become more commonplace.

(A) highly
(B) gradually
(C) frequently
(D) properly

016. Ⓐ Ⓑ Ⓒ Ⓓ
017. Ⓐ Ⓑ Ⓒ Ⓓ
018. Ⓐ Ⓑ Ⓒ Ⓓ
019. Ⓐ Ⓑ Ⓒ Ⓓ

副詞01

選択肢

(A) highly 副 非常に   (B) gradually 副 徐々に、だんだんと

(C) frequently 副 頻繁に   (D) properly 副 適切に、正しく

正解・訳

016. **(D)**

会議室の全ての機器が適切に動作していることを、お客様が到着する前に確認してください。

017. **(C)**

わが社の販売員は、顧客から頻繁に聞かれる質問に答えられるようにトレーニングを受けている。

018. **(A)**

Corecoms Industries Inc. は、研究開発チームに加わる非常にやる気のあるエンジニアを探している。

019. **(B)**

ここ数年の間に、オフィス用品をオンラインで購入することが徐々に当たり前のことになってきた。

commonplace: 当たり前のこと

解説

016 の work properly（適切に動作する）や **018** の highly motivated（非常にやる気のある）は TOEIC に頻出のフレーズだ。**017** は frequently asked questions（よくある質問）という定型表現がポイントになる。**019** の gradually は完了形の間に入り「徐々に〜になった」という意味。

もう1問！

020. Corecoms Industries Inc. is looking for highly ------- engineers to join our research and development team.

    (A) activated (B) assigned (C) motivated (D) urbanized

▶▶▶ 解答は033ページ

Unit 1
Set 5

021. You may use a credit card statement as proof of purchase ------- you lose your receipt.

022. According to the site manager, it does not look ------- the construction project will be completed on time.

023. We will take a coffee break at 3 P.M. ------- we are running out of time.

024. The hotel got an excellent review ------- its restaurant did not rate nearly as highly.

(A) whereas
(B) unless
(C) in the event that
(D) as if

021. Ⓐ Ⓑ Ⓒ Ⓓ
022. Ⓐ Ⓑ Ⓒ Ⓓ
023. Ⓐ Ⓑ Ⓒ Ⓓ
024. Ⓐ Ⓑ Ⓒ Ⓓ

接続詞01

選択肢

(A) whereas [接] 〜だが、ところが　　　(B) unless [接] 〜でない限り

(C) in the event that （万一）〜の場合には　　　(D) as if 〜のようだ

正解・訳

021. (C)

万一レシートを紛失してしまった場合には、クレジットカードの明細書を購入の証明
として使うことができます。

statement: 取引明細書

022. (D)

現場監督によると、建築プロジェクトは予定通りには終わらないようだ。

023. (B)

時間が足りなくならない限り、午後3時に小休憩を取る。

run out of 〜: 〜が足りなくなる

024. (A)

ホテルは素晴らしいという評価を得たが、そのレストランはそれほど高く評価されな
かった。

rate: 評価される、〜と見積もられる

解説

接続表現が並んでいる。**021**のin the event that 〜（万一〜の場合には）は、条件を表す
接続表現。ifよりも実現の可能性が低い場合に用いられる。**022**のlook as if 〜は後に未
来形や現在形の節を伴い、「〜のようだ」という表現。**024**のwhereasは「だが」という
意味でwhileとほぼ同意だが、やや硬い対比の表現だ。

もう1問！

025. You may use a credit card statement as ------- of purchase in the
event that you lose your receipt.

(A) proof　(B) credibility　(C) choice　(D) promise

▶▶▶ 解答は033ページ

Unit 1
Set 6

026. Bellevue Restaurant asks each ------- to fill out a customer satisfaction survey after the meal.

027. There is an opening for a computer ------- at Jenkins Networking Solutions.

028. According to company policy, a sales ------- must welcome guests at the airport when they arrive.

029. As a ------- of Greendale, you are entitled to dispose of garbage at the recycling center free of charge.

(A) diner
(B) representative
(C) technician
(D) resident

026. Ⓐ Ⓑ Ⓒ Ⓓ
027. Ⓐ Ⓑ Ⓒ Ⓓ
028. Ⓐ Ⓑ Ⓒ Ⓓ
029. Ⓐ Ⓑ Ⓒ Ⓓ

名詞02

選択肢

(A) diner　名 食事客
(B) representative　名 販売員、代表者
(C) technician　名 技術者
(D) resident　名 住人

正解・訳

026. (A)

Bellevue Restaurant では、食事客それぞれに、食事の後に顧客満足度調査に記入するよう頼んでいる。
survey: 調査

027. (C)

Jenkins Networking Solutions では、コンピューター技術者の職に空きがある。

028. (B)

会社の方針によると、営業部員は顧客が空港に着いた時に出迎えなければならない。
sales representative: 営業部員、販売員

029. (D)

Greendaleの住人として、あなたはゴミを無料でリサイクリングセンターに捨てる権利があります。
be entitled to: ～する権利がある／dispose of ~: ～を捨てる

解説

職種など、人を指す名詞が並んでいる。**026**のdinerは食事客を指す。ちなみに、動詞の形はdineで「食事をする」という意味だ。**027**と**028**は空所の直前に名詞があるので、それらと相性が良い語を探す。**027**はsales representative（営業担当者）、**028**はcomputer technician（コンピューター技術者）という頻出表現を素早く見抜けるかどうかが鍵。

もう１問！

030. As a resident of Greendale, you are ------- to dispose of garbage at the recycling center free of charge.

(A) enlightened　(B) rushed　(C) tempted　(D) entitled

▶▶▶ 解答は034ページ

Unit 1
Set 7

031. Ms. Smith was praised for her ability to ------- her job perfectly even at the busiest times of year.

032. Hobart brand furniture items are easy to ------- with only a screwdriver.

033. The advisors from Busincorp have helped many small businesses ------- themselves and grow into thriving companies.

034. To ------- a renovation permit from the city, construction companies are required to submit a comprehensive proposal.

(A) establish
(B) obtain
(C) perform
(D) assemble

031. Ⓐ Ⓑ Ⓒ Ⓓ
032. Ⓐ Ⓑ Ⓒ Ⓓ
033. Ⓐ Ⓑ Ⓒ Ⓓ
034. Ⓐ Ⓑ Ⓒ Ⓓ

動詞02

選択肢

(A) establish 動 〜を創立する、〜を確立する　(B) obtain 動 〜を手に入れる
(C) perform 動 〜（役割など）を果たす　(D) assemble 動 〜を組み立てる

正解・訳

031. (C)
Smithさんは1年中で最も忙しい時期でも完璧に職務を果たす能力を称賛された。

032. (D)
Hobartブランドの家具はドライバーだけで簡単に組み立てることができる。

033. (A)
Busincorpのアドバイザーは、多くの小企業が創業し、繁栄するまでに成長するのを助けた。
establish oneself: 開業する

034. (B)
改築の許可証を市から入手するために、建築会社は包括的な提案書の提出をすることが求められる。
comprehensive: 包括的な、全体的な

解説

空所の後にある語句と相性の良い動詞を選ぶのがコツ。**031**は空所後にher job（彼女の仕事）があるため、perform（〜を果たす）が適切。**033**のestablishは他動詞で、再帰代名詞を伴うと「創業する、開業する」という意味になる。**034**はobtain A from B（BからAを入手する）という表現を見抜きたい。

もう1問！

035. Ms. Smith was praised for her ability to perform her job ------- even at the busiest times of year.

(A) especially　(B) automatically　(C) recklessly　(D) perfectly

▶▶▶ 解答は034ページ

Unit 1
Set 8

036. C&S Luxury Condominiums boast ------- balconies separated by bamboo partitions.

037. The blueprint for the building is complete apart from some ------- adjustments that have been requested.

038. Mr. Clemens has hired some ------- decorators to modernize the San Francisco office.

039. The ------- design for the Clarendon Seafood Restaurant logo featured an octopus rather than a crab.

(A) private
(B) interior
(C) minor
(D) original

036. Ⓐ Ⓑ Ⓒ Ⓓ
037. Ⓐ Ⓑ Ⓒ Ⓓ
038. Ⓐ Ⓑ Ⓒ Ⓓ
039. Ⓐ Ⓑ Ⓒ Ⓓ

形容詞02

....
(A) private 形 個別の、個人の (B) interior 形 内部の、インテリアの

(C) minor 形 小さな、重要でない (D) original 形 最初の

正解・訳
....

036. (A)

C&S Luxury Condominiumsは、竹製のしきりで隔てられた<u>個別の</u>バルコニーを備えている。

boast: (誇りになるものとして)〜を持っている

037. (C)

ビルの設計図は、要求があった<u>小さな</u>修正点を除いては完成した。

apart from 〜: 〜を除けば

038. (B)

Clemensさんは San Francisco の支所を現代的にするために<u>インテリア</u>デザイナーを雇った。

039. (D)

Clarendon Seafood Restaurantの<u>最初の</u>ロゴは、カニではなくタコを中心に据えていた。

feature: 〜を特徴とする、主役とする

解説
....

空所後の名詞と相性が良い形容詞を選ぶ。**036**は文の後半の説明から、private balcony (個別のバルコニー) であると判断する。**037**のminor adjustmentsは「小さな修正、ちょっとした修正」という意味。「大幅な修正」ならばmajor adjustmentsだ。**038**は interior decorators (インテリアデザイナー) という固まりを見抜けるかが鍵。

もう1問！
....

040. Mr. Clemens has hired some interior decorators to ------- the San Francisco office.

(A) maximize (B) specialize (C) modernize (D) recognize

▶▶▶ 解答は034ページ

Unit 1
Set 9

041. Mr. Peters lived in Edinburgh for many years until ------- moving to Delhi.

042. Alnwicks' outdoor benches are vinyl-coated and can be ------- cleaned with a cloth dampened with water.

043. Fan Ju Hotel is located ------- in the center of town, within walking distance of public transportation.

044. Due to heavier than usual traffic, Mr. Hammond ------- missed his flight from Heathrow Airport.

   (A) conveniently
   (B) easily
   (C) nearly
   (D) recently

041.	Ⓐ Ⓑ Ⓒ Ⓓ
042.	Ⓐ Ⓑ Ⓒ Ⓓ
043.	Ⓐ Ⓑ Ⓒ Ⓓ
044.	Ⓐ Ⓑ Ⓒ Ⓓ

副詞02

選択肢

(A) conveniently　副 便利に、都合良く　　(B) easily　副 簡単に、たやすく

(C) nearly　副 もう少しで、危うく　　(D) recently　副 最近

正解・訳

041. (D)
Petersさんは、最近Delhiに引っ越すまで長年Edinburghに住んでいた。

042. (B)
Alnwicksの屋外ベンチはビニールコーティングされており、水を含ませた布で簡単に掃除することができる。

043. (A)
Fan Ju Hotelは、公共交通機関から歩いて行ける街の中心部に便利に位置している。

044. (C)
普段よりも交通量が多かったため、HammondさんはHeathrow空港からのフライトにもう少しで乗り遅れるところだった。

解説

041のuntil recently（最近まで）はTOEICに頻出する表現なので、フレーズで覚えておきたい。043はconveniently located（便利な場所にある）という語順でもよく出る。044はnearly missedで「危うく乗り遅れそうになったが、ぎりぎりで間に合った」ということ。「乗り遅れた」と誤解しやすいので注意。

もう1問！

045. Due to ------- than usual traffic, Mr. Hammond nearly missed his flight from Heathrow Airport.

　　(A) more　(B) earlier　(C) faster　(D) heavier

▶▶▶ 解答は034ページ

学習日 / / /

問題046-050 Unit 1

Unit 1
Set 10

046. The warehouse ------- located on Ellerton Road was thoroughly cleaned for inspection the next day.

047. There has been a huge ------- in the number of accidents since Maxine Winthrop took over as factory manager.

048. Some vacant stores on the first floor will be reconstructed to make ------- for the mall's new food court.

049. Atlanta's Belvedere Bank is a well-known financial ------- that has been in business for more than 100 years.

(A) room
(B) facility
(C) institution
(D) reduction

046. Ⓐ Ⓑ Ⓒ Ⓓ
047. Ⓐ Ⓑ Ⓒ Ⓓ
048. Ⓐ Ⓑ Ⓒ Ⓓ
049. Ⓐ Ⓑ Ⓒ Ⓓ

名詞03

(A) room 名 場所、空間、部屋　(B) facility 名 施設、設備
(C) institution 名 (特殊な目的を持つ) 機関、施設
(D) reduction 名 減少、削減

正解・訳

046. (B)
Ellerton Roadにある倉庫施設は、次の日の点検のために徹底的に清掃された。
thoroughly: 徹底的に／inspection: 点検、検査

047. (D)
Maxine Winthropが工場長の職に就いてから、事故の件数が大幅に減少した。

048. (A)
1階にあるいくつかの空き店舗は、ショッピングモールの新しいフードコートの場所を
つくるために建て替えられる。

049. (C)
AtlantaのBelvedere Bankは100年以上にわたって営業している有名な金融機関である。

解説

046と**049**はwarehouse facility (倉庫施設) とfinancial institution (金融機関) という名詞
の固まりを想起して即答したい。また、空所後の前置詞に着目して、**047**のreduction
in ~ (~の減少) や**048**のmake room for ~ (~のための場所をつくる) という定型表現を
見抜くことも重要だ。

もう1問！

050. Some vacant stores on the first floor will be ------- to make room for
the mall's new food court.
　　　　(A) reconstructed　(B) subdued　(C) postponed　(D) installed

▶▶▶ 解答は034ページ

Unit 1
Set 11

051. Having earned her license last year, Ms. Tai is
------- to work as an accountant.

052. The interviewers were ------- with the answers
Ms. Davis gave at her interview and will probably
offer her the position.

053. Over the past 20 years, Ms. Tanaka has -------
herself to the Sutton Wildlife Protection Agency.

054. At the upcoming community luncheon, Ms. Winters
will be ------- for her commitment to preserve local
historic sites.

(A) qualified
(B) impressed
(C) dedicated
(D) recognized

051. Ⓐ Ⓑ Ⓒ Ⓓ
052. Ⓐ Ⓑ Ⓒ Ⓓ
053. Ⓐ Ⓑ Ⓒ Ⓓ
054. Ⓐ Ⓑ Ⓒ Ⓓ

動詞03

選択肢

(A) qualified 　動 ～の資格を与えた、適格とした　形 資格のある

(B) impressed 　動 ～に感銘を与えた

(C) dedicated 　動 ～に専念した、～に打ち込んだ

(D) recognized 　動 ～を表彰した、～(功績など)を認めた

正解・訳

051. (A)

昨年免許を取得したので、Tai さんは会計士として働く資格を持っている。

052. (B)

面接官は Davis さんの面接での返答に感銘を受けたので、おそらく彼女にその職をオファーするだろう。

053. (C)

過去20年の間、Tanaka さんは Sutton 野生保護局での仕事に打ち込んできた。

054. (D)

今度の地域の昼食会で、Winters さんは地元の史跡を保存するための取り組みに対して表彰される。

commitment: 取り組み、献身

解説

空所後にある語が手掛かりになる。**052** は be impressed with ～(～に感銘を受ける)とすると文意が通る。**053** は空所後の herself という再帰代名詞に着目。dedicate oneself to ～で「～に打ち込む」という成句だ。**054** は recognize A for B(B に対する A の功績を認める)の受け身の形。

もう1問！

055. Having ------- her license last year, Ms. Tai is qualified to work as a certified public accountant.

(A) earned　(B) operated　(C) dismissed　(D) enlarged

▶▶▶ 解答は034ページ

Unit 1 　もう1問！ 解答一覧

※問題文の訳は(→ 　)内のページ・番号を参照してください

005. (C)

There is an additional charge when passengers bring ------- item on Stuart Air's discount flight.

(A) exaggerated 　動 誇張された 　　　(B) spread 　動 広がった
(C) oversized 　動 サイズが超過した 　(D) customized 　動 注文通りに作られた

(→ p. 12、**001**)

010. (A)

At Bearing Entertainment, we are always striving to produce high-quality content to fulfill our viewers' ------- .

(A) expectations 　名 期待 　　　(B) celebrations 　名 お祝い
(C) regulations 　名 規則 　　　　(D) reputations 　名 評判

(→ p. 14、**008**)

015. (B)

The Summer Breeze Spa provides personalized treatments to ------- your individual needs.

(A) react 　動 ～に反応する 　(B) suit 　動 ～を満足させる
(C) cater 　動 応える 　　　　(D) take 　動 取る

(→ p. 16、**012**)

020. (C)

Corecoms Industries Inc. is looking for highly ------- engineers to join our research and development team.

(A) activated 　形 活性化された 　(B) assigned 　形 割り当てられた
(C) motivated 　形 やる気のある 　(D) urbanized 　形 都会化された

(→ p. 18、**018**)

025. (A)

You may use a credit card statement as ------- of purchase in the event that you lose your receipt.

(A) proof 　名 証明 　　(B) credibility 　名 信頼性
(C) choice 　名 選択 　　(D) promise 　名 約束

(→ p. 20、**021**)

030. (D)

As a resident of Greendale, you are ------- to dispose of garbage at the recycling center free of charge.

(A) enlightened 　動 啓発した
(B) rushed 　動 急いだ
(C) tempted 　動 そそのかした
(D) entitled 　動 権利を与えた

(→ p. 22、**029**)

035. (D)

Ms. Smith was praised for her ability to perform her job ------- even at the busiest times of year.

(A) especially 　副 特に
(B) automatically 　副 自動的に
(C) recklessly 　副 無謀に
(D) perfectly 　副 完全に

(→ p. 24、**031**)

040. (C)

Mr. Clemens has hired some interior decorators to ------- the San Francisco office.

(A) maximize 　動 最大化する
(B) specialize 　動 専門に追求する
(C) modernize 　動 近代化する
(D) recognize 　動 認める

(→ p. 26、**038**)

045. (D)

Due to ------- than usual traffic, Mr. Hammond nearly missed his flight from Heathrow Airport.

(A) more 　形 より多い
(B) earlier 　形 より早い
(C) faster 　形 より速い
(D) heavier 　形 より重い、より大量の

(→ p. 28、**044**)

050. (A)

Some vacant stores on the first floor will be ------- to make room for the mall's new food court.

(A) reconstructed 　動 建築し直した
(B) subdued 　動 やわらいだ、抑えた
(C) postponed 　動 延期した
(D) installed 　動 据え付けた

(→ p. 30、**048**)

055. (A)

Having ------- her license last year, Ms. Tai is qualified to work as a certified public accountant.

(A) earned 　動 獲得した
(B) operated 　動 管理した、運営した
(C) dismissed 　動 却下した
(D) enlarged 　動 拡大した

(→ p. 32、**051**)

Unit 2
Set 1

056. In ------- to all of the other branches, the Fielding office has had strong sales this month.

057. Despite the very talented ------- , Samantha Ellis won first place at the annual photography contest in Brisbane.

058. Due to a scheduling ------- , Ms. Chang was unable to attend the monthly section meeting.

059. Thompson Motors is a used car dealer that specializes in classic cars in excellent ------- .

(A) conflict
(B) contrast
(C) condition
(D) competition

056. Ⓐ Ⓑ Ⓒ Ⓓ
057. Ⓐ Ⓑ Ⓒ Ⓓ
058. Ⓐ Ⓑ Ⓒ Ⓓ
059. Ⓐ Ⓑ Ⓒ Ⓓ

名詞04

選択肢

(A) conflict 名 衝突、不一致　　(B) contrast 名 対照

(C) condition 名 状態　　(D) competition 名 競争相手、競争

正解・訳

056. (B)

他の支社とは対照的に、Fielding支社の今月の売り上げは好調だった。

057. (D)

才能がある競争相手がいたにもかかわらず、Samantha EllisはBrisbaneでの毎年恒例の写真コンテストで1位を獲得した。

058. (A)

スケジュールの衝突のため、Changさんは月例の部会に出席することができなかった。

059. (C)

Thompson Motorsは状態が非常に良いクラシックカーを専門に扱う中古車販売ディーラーである。

specialize in ~: ～を専門とする

解説

051のin contrast to ~（～と対照的に）は対比を表すTOEIC頻出表現。**052**のcompetition（競争相手）は人を表す名詞としても使われるので、空所の前のtalented（才能がある）に説明される語として適切。**053**のscheduling conflictは「スケジュールがかぶること」というフレーズとして覚えたい。

もう1問！

060. Thompson Motors is a used car dealer that ------- in classic cars in excellent condition.

(A) restores (B) specializes (C) utilizes (D) recommends

▶▶▶ 解答は057ページ

Unit 2
Set 2

061. The council has ------- a number of suggestions regarding the use of the site of the old firehouse.

062. Because the delays at the factory ------- , clients were given the option of canceling their orders.

063. Your reservation for one night's stay at Newport Inn has been ------- .

064. A contact number is ------- before your order can be processed by the shipping department.

(A) confirmed
(B) required
(C) persisted
(D) accepted

061. Ⓐ Ⓑ Ⓒ Ⓓ
062. Ⓐ Ⓑ Ⓒ Ⓓ
063. Ⓐ Ⓑ Ⓒ Ⓓ
064. Ⓐ Ⓑ Ⓒ Ⓓ

動詞04

選択肢

(A) confirmed　動 ～を確認した　　(B) required　動 ～を要求した

(C) persisted　動 続いた　　(D) accepted　動 ～を受け入れた

正解・訳

061. (D)

議会は古い消防署の用地の利用法について多くの提案を受け入れた。

council:（地方自治体の）議会

062. (C)

工場での遅れが続いたため、顧客は注文をキャンセルするという選択肢を与えられた。

063. (A)

あなたのNewport Innでの1泊の予約が確認されました。

064. (B)

あなたの注文が発送担当部によって処理される前に、連絡先の電話番号が必要です。

process: ～を処理する

解説

選択肢には動詞が並んでいるので、主語や目的語との関係に着目する。**062**の空所の後には目的語がないので、自動詞のpersist（～が続く）が語法の観点からも適切。**063**はconfirm a reservation（予約を確認する）という表現の受け身の形だ。TOEICには頻出の表現なので、フレーズで覚えておきたい。

もう1問！

065. Because the delays at the factory persisted, clients were ------- the option of canceling their orders.

(A) selected　(B) chosen　(C) preferred　(D) given

▶▶▶ 解答は057ページ

Unit 2
Set 3

066. With a background in theater, Ms. Jamil proved to be a truly ------- addition to the production team.

067. The purchasing officer is ------- for the quality of all products that arrive from overseas suppliers.

068. Sales of Tyrion Electronics' new tablet computer have improved for four ------- months.

069. The customer satisfaction surveys revealed ------- ways in which the company can improve its service.

(A) consecutive
(B) numerous
(C) accountable
(D) invaluable

066. Ⓐ Ⓑ Ⓒ Ⓓ
067. Ⓐ Ⓑ Ⓒ Ⓓ
068. Ⓐ Ⓑ Ⓒ Ⓓ
069. Ⓐ Ⓑ Ⓒ Ⓓ

形容詞03

選択肢

(A) consecutive 　形 連続の、連続した　(B) numerous 　形 多数の、たくさんの
(C) accountable 　形 責任がある　(D) invaluable 　形 貴重な

正解・訳

066. (D)

演劇の経験があるため、Jamilさんは制作チームにとって本当に貴重な新人であることが分かった。
prove to be ~: ~であると分かる／addition: 加わった人、新人

067. (C)

購買部長は、海外の供給業者から来た全ての製品の品質に責任がある。

068. (A)

Tyrion Electronicsの新しいタブレットコンピューターの売り上げは4カ月連続で改善した。

069. (B)

顧客満足度調査は、会社がサービスを改善するための多数の方法を明らかにした。

解説

067のaccountable for ~は「~に責任がある」という意味。ちなみに動詞の形はaccountで、account for ~(~を説明する)のように使う。**068**のconsecutiveは「数字+ consecutive +時間の単位」(~の間連続して)という形で用いられる頻出表現だ。**069**はnumerous (多数の)を入れればnumerous ways (多数の方法)となり文意が通る。

もう1問！

070. The customer satisfaction surveys ------- numerous ways in which the company can improve its service.

(A) extended　(B) revealed　(C) inquired　(D) prompted

▶▶▶ 解答は057ページ

Unit 2

Set 4

071. Please be sure to be ------- the train by 1:00 P.M. as it will leave shortly thereafter.

072. Riverside County Book Fair was well-attended by locals and tourists ------- .

073. When Mr. Kym stepped ------- as senior sales representative, Marla Hernandez took his place.

074. The central office and the warehouse are only about 100 meters ------- , which is quite convenient.

(A) aside
(B) alike
(C) apart
(D) aboard

071. Ⓐ Ⓑ Ⓒ Ⓓ
072. Ⓐ Ⓑ Ⓒ Ⓓ
073. Ⓐ Ⓑ Ⓒ Ⓓ
074. Ⓐ Ⓑ Ⓒ Ⓓ

選択肢

(A) aside 　副　脇に、傍らに 　　　(B) alike 　副　同様に

(C) apart 　副　離れて 　　　(D) aboard 　前　副　〜に乗って

正解・訳

071. (D)

その後すぐに出発するので、午後1時までには電車に乗っているようにしてください。
thereafter: その後

072. (B)

Riverside County ブックフェアは、地元の人も旅行客も同様に大勢の参加者があった。
well-attended: 参加者の多い

073. (A)

Kym さんが上級の営業担当者の地位から身を引いた時、Marla Hernandez が彼の代わり
を務めた。
step aside: (地位などから) 身を引く／take ~'s place: 〜の代わりを務める

074. (C)

中央オフィスと倉庫はほんの100メートルしか離れておらず、とても便利である。

解説

071のaboardは、Welcome aboard.（ご乗車ありがとうございます）という表現でリスニングにも頻出。**072**はA and B alike（AもBも同様に）という成句が見抜いて即答できるようにしたい。**073**の空所にasideを入れ、step aside as ~（〜から身を引く）とすると、文意も通る。**074**の(C) apartは距離・時間の表現＋apartで「〜だけ離れて」という意味。

もう1問！

075. Please be sure to be aboard the train by 1:00 P.M. as it will leave
------- thereafter.

(A) possibly (B) slowly (C) shortly (D) timely

▶▶▶ 解答は057ページ

Unit 2

Set 5

076. Around 500 guests will attend the concert ------- the Osman Concert Hall.

077. The furniture in Ms. Anderson's office consists ------- a wooden desk and a leather executive chair.

078. All payments for online purchases must be made ------- credit card.

079. The successful candidate will be familiar ------- various types of social networking applications.

(A) at
(B) with
(C) by
(D) of

076. Ⓐ Ⓑ Ⓒ Ⓓ
077. Ⓐ Ⓑ Ⓒ Ⓓ
078. Ⓐ Ⓑ Ⓒ Ⓓ
079. Ⓐ Ⓑ Ⓒ Ⓓ

前置詞01

選択肢

(A) at 前 ～(場所、時間)で   (B) with 前 ～と共に

(C) by 前 ～によって   (D) of 前 ～の、～から成る

正解・訳

076. (A)

約500人の観客がOsman Concert Hall<u>で</u>のコンサートに行く。

077. (D)

Andersonさんのオフィスの家具は木製の机と革張りの重役椅子<u>から</u>成っている。

consist of ~: ～から成る

078. (C)

オンラインでの買い物の支払いは、全てクレジットカード<u>で</u>されなければならない。

079. (B)

採用される候補者は、さまざまなタイプのソーシャル・ネットワーキングのアプリ<u>に</u>精通している人である。

解説

076のatは場所を表す前置詞で、コンサート会場などの具体的な場所を表す名詞の前で用いられる。**077**のofは「～の (一部)」という意味で、動詞consitを伴いconsist of ~ (～から成る)という表現を作る。**078**のbyは支払いの手段を表す前置詞。**079**のfamiliar with ~ (～を熟知している)は頻出表現なので、ぜひフレーズで押さえておきたい。

もう1問！

080. The ------- candidate will be familiar with various types of social networking applications.

(A) spontaneous (B) hopeful (C) constant (D) successful

▶▶▶ 解答は057ページ

Unit 2

Set 6

081. Interested people are advised to double-check the job ------- before applying.

082. The marketing manager expressed a strong ------- for holding the product launch on Wednesday.

083. Realtors at Urban District Real Estate receive a 6 percent ------- on all residential property sales.

084. Ms. Briton was given an award for her outstanding contribution to the museum's fundraising ------- .

(A) preference
(B) initiative
(C) commission
(D) description

081. Ⓐ Ⓑ Ⓒ Ⓓ
082. Ⓐ Ⓑ Ⓒ Ⓓ
083. Ⓐ Ⓑ Ⓒ Ⓓ
084. Ⓐ Ⓑ Ⓒ Ⓓ

名詞05

選択肢

(A) preference 名 (選択の) 好み、(for 〜で) 〜の希望

(B) initiative 名 計画、新しい試み   (C) commission 名 手数料、委託

(D) description 名 説明、記述

正解・訳

081. (D)

興味がある人は、応募する前に職務内容説明書を再確認するように勧められている。

082. (A)

マーケティング部長は、水曜日に製品を発売したいという強い希望を表明した。

083. (C)

Urban District Real Estateで働く不動産業者は、全ての居住用財産の販売につき6パーセントの手数料を受け取る。

084. (B)

Britonさんは、博物館の資金集め計画に対するずばぬけた貢献に対して賞を授与された。

解説

081のjob description (職務内容説明書) は固まりで覚えておきたい。**083**のcommissionには「手数料」という名詞の他に「(職務など) を委託する」という意味の動詞もある。(B)のinitiativeには「計画」という意味があり、**084**のfund raising initiativeは「資金集めの計画」。

もう1問！

085. Ms. Briton was given an award for her ------- contribution to the museum's fundraising initiative.

(A) outstanding (B) trivial (C) credential (D) humid

▶▶▶ 解答は058ページ

Unit 2
Set 7

086. If you would like to upgrade your computer, you should ------- a request with a supervisor.

087. Please visit our Web site to ------- out more about the special exhibition featuring local painters.

088. On their first day at Cooper Plumbing, employees are sent to the general affairs office to ------- out some forms.

089. The advertising campaign for Nova Motors' new forklift will ------- on the company's reputation for dependability.

(A) fill
(B) file
(C) find
(D) focus

086. Ⓐ Ⓑ Ⓒ Ⓓ
087. Ⓐ Ⓑ Ⓒ Ⓓ
088. Ⓐ Ⓑ Ⓒ Ⓓ
089. Ⓐ Ⓑ Ⓒ Ⓓ

動詞05

選択肢

(A) fill 動 ～に記入する　　　　　　(B) file 動 （書類など）を提出する
(C) find 動 ～を見つけ出す、～を知る (D) focus 動 重点を置く

正解・訳

086. (B)
コンピューターをアップグレードしたいならば、上司に申請書を提出するべきだ。

087. (C)
地元のアーティストを特集した展示会についての情報を知るにはウェブサイトをご覧ください。

088. (A)
従業員は、Cooper Plumbingでの最初の就業日に、数種類の書類に記入するために総務部に行くよう指示される。

089. (D)
Nova Motorsの新しいフォークリフトの宣伝キャンペーンは、同社の信頼度が高いという評判に焦点を当てる。

解説

086はfile a requestで「申請書を提出する」という定番のフレーズ。submit a requestもほぼ同意。**087**、**088**、**089**は空所後の前置詞や副詞に着目し、それぞれ文意が通るようにfind out ~（～を見つける）、fill out ~（～に記入する）、focus on ~（～に重点を置く）という句動詞を作る語を入れる。

もう1問！

090. The advertising campaign for Nova Motors' new forklift will focus on the company's ------- for dependability.

(A) nomination (B) reputation (C) identification (D) participation

▶▶▶ 解答は058ページ

Unit 2
Set 8

091. Liang Bi has received the ------- Zenith Award for her research into new energy storage solutions.

092. The CEO of Peterson Shoes stepped down, saying it was time for a younger leader to make the company more ------- and dynamic.

093. The engineers at Giodani Constructions conducted a ------- review of the bridge plans to ensure there would be no structural problems.

094. The Kaigangi Botanical Garden features wildflowers and trees that are ------- to the region.

(A) meticulous
(B) indigenous
(C) vibrant
(D) prestigious

091. Ⓐ Ⓑ Ⓒ Ⓓ
092. Ⓐ Ⓑ Ⓒ Ⓓ
093. Ⓐ Ⓑ Ⓒ Ⓓ
094. Ⓐ Ⓑ Ⓒ Ⓓ

形容詞04

選択肢

(A) meticulous 　形 厳密な、細部にまで気を配る
(B) indigenous 　形 自生している
(C) vibrant 　形 活気に満ちた　　　(D) prestigious 　形 名声のある

正解・訳

091. (D)

Liang Bi は、彼女の新しいエネルギー貯蔵法の研究について<u>名声のある</u>Zenith Award を受賞した。

092. (C)

Peterson Shoes のCEO は、より若いリーダーが、会社をより<u>活気に満ちた</u>力強いものにする時であると言い、職を退いた。

093. (A)

Giodani Constructions のエンジニアたちは、構造的な問題がないことを保証するために橋の設計図の<u>厳密な</u>見直しを行った。
plan: 設計図／structural: 構造的な

094. (B)

Kaigangi 植物園は、その地方に<u>自生している</u>野草や木を呼び物にしている。

解説

091 の prestigious award は「名高い賞、格式の高い賞」を指す。**092** は and の後の dynamic （ダイナミックな）と並列関係になる語として vibrant （活力に満ちた）が適切。**093** は meticulous review で「厳密な見直し」となり文意が通る。**094** の空所後にある前置詞 to と相性が良いのは (B) indigenous で、indigenous to ~ は「~に自生している」を意味する。

もう1問！

095. The engineers at Giodani Constructions ------- a meticulous review of the bridge plans to ensure there would be no structural problems.

(A) committed　(B) registered　(C) indicated　(D) conducted

▶▶▶ 解答は058ページ

Unit 2

Set 9

096. The board of directors has not ------- decided which supplier to rely on for our employee uniforms.

097. There are ------- tickets available for Judith White's concert on Friday night although Saturday's event is sold out.

098. The construction crew lost ------- three days to bad weather and managed to finish by the agreed date.

099. Denning Street, in central Morrisdale, is one of the ------- desirable business addresses for accounting and legal firms.

(A) only
(B) still
(C) most
(D) yet

096. Ⓐ Ⓑ Ⓒ Ⓓ
097. Ⓐ Ⓑ Ⓒ Ⓓ
098. Ⓐ Ⓑ Ⓒ Ⓓ
099. Ⓐ Ⓑ Ⓒ Ⓓ

副詞04

選択肢

(A) only 副 ～だけ   (B) still 副 まだ

(C) most 副 最も   (D) yet 副 (否定文で) まだ～ない

正解・訳

096. (D)

取締役会は、従業員の制服をどの供給会社に頼むのかを<u>まだ</u>決めていない。

supplier: 供給会社

097. (B)

土曜日のイベントは売り切れたが、金曜日の夜のJudith Whiteのコンサートチケットは<u>まだ</u>入手可能である。

available: 入手可能な

098. (A)

建設作業員たちは悪天候下でも3日<u>しか</u>遅れることなく、合意された日までに何とか作業を終えた。

manage to ~: 何とか～する

099. (C)

Morrisdale中心部のDenning Streetは会計事務所や法律事務所には<u>最も</u>好ましい住所の1つである。

desirable: 好ましい

解説

096のhave notと過去分詞の間の空所は、yet (まだ～ない) の定位置の1つだ。**097**は文の後半から「まだチケットがある」と分かるため、(B) のstillが適切。**099**は後半でone of the ~ (～の1つ) という最上級の前に置かれる定番表現があるので、最上級を作るmostを使いthe most desirable (最も好ましい) とする。

もう1問!

100. Denning Street, in central Morrisdale, is one of the most ------- business addresses for accounting and legal firms.

(A) manageable   (B) durable   (C) desirable   (D) comparable

▶▶▶ 解答は058ページ

Unit 2
Set 10

101. Mr. Patel has sat on the board of directors of a number of well-known nonprofit ------- .

102. According to city regulations, ------- under 25 meters in height are not required to have elevators.

103. The communication skills workshop will be held at our corporate ------- in Mumbai.

104. Applicants for the art director position must submit ------- , which will be returned at the interview.

(A) structures
(B) portfolios
(C) headquarters
(D) organizations

101. Ⓐ Ⓑ Ⓒ Ⓓ
102. Ⓐ Ⓑ Ⓒ Ⓓ
103. Ⓐ Ⓑ Ⓒ Ⓓ
104. Ⓐ Ⓑ Ⓒ Ⓓ

名詞06

選択肢

(A) structure 名 建造物、構造 (B) portfolio 名 (業績を示すための)作品集

(C) headquarters 名 本社 (D) organizations 名 組織、団体

正解・訳

101. (D)

Patel さんは数々の有名な非営利団体の理事を務めてきた。

sit on: ~(理事会など)の一員である

102. (A)

市の新しい規則によると、高さが25メートル未満の建造物にはエレベーターは必須ではない。

regulation: 規則

103. (C)

コミュニケーションスキルのワークショップは、Mumbaiの本社で行われる。

104. (B)

アートディレクターの職に応募する者は作品集を提出する必要があり、それは面接の時に返却される。

解説

(A)のstructureは、ビルから物置小屋まで大小さまざまな建築物を指す語として頻出。(B)のportfolio(作品集)は、Part 7の求人広告やPart 2の会話に頻出する単語なので、ぜひ覚えておきたい。(C)のheadquartersは単数でも語尾にsが付くことに注意。

もう1問!

105. ------- for the art director position must submit portfolios, which will be returned at the interview.

    (A) Applicants (B) Recipients (C) Advocates (D) Interns

▶▶▶ 解答は058ページ

Unit 2
Set 11

106. Dr. Johnson could not ------- it to the medical conference due to a scheduling issue.

107. The factory machinery is aging, and it has become necessary to perform daily maintenance to ensure that it will ------- smoothly.

108. Before you ------- an order for ink cartridges, please double-check the model number of your printer.

109. For immediate assistance, please ------- our technical support staff.

(A) place
(B) make
(C) call
(D) run

106. Ⓐ Ⓑ Ⓒ Ⓓ
107. Ⓐ Ⓑ Ⓒ Ⓓ
108. Ⓐ Ⓑ Ⓒ Ⓓ
109. Ⓐ Ⓑ Ⓒ Ⓓ

選択肢

(A) place 　動 ～（注文）をする

(B) make 　動 ～に到着する、（make it で）～に間に合う

(C) call 　動 ～に電話をかける 　　(D) run 　動 （機械などが）作動する、動く

正解・訳

106. (B)

Johnson医師は、スケジュールの問題で医学学会に間に合わなかった。

107. (D)

工場の機械は老朽化しており、それらがスムーズに作動することを確実にするために日々のメンテナンスをすることが必須になっている。

108. (A)

インクカートリッジの注文をする前に、プリンターの型番を再確認してください。

109. (C)

すぐにサポートを受けるには、テクニカルサポート係にお電話ください。

解説

106は空所後にitがあることから、make it（～に間に合う）というイディオムを想起し即答したい。**107**のrunは「（機械など）が作動する」という意味でsmoothlyと相性が良い。**108**のplace an order（注文する）という成句はTOEICの全てのパートで頻出する。**109**のようにテクニカルサポートに電話をかけるのはTOEICでは定番のシナリオだ。

もう1問！

110. The factory ------- is aging, and it has become necessary to perform daily maintenance to ensure that it will run smoothly.

(A) workplace　(B) mechanic　(C) technology　(D) machinery

▶▶▶ 解答は058ページ

Unit 2 もう1問！ 解答一覧

※問題文の訳は(→)内のページ・番号を参照してください

060. (B)

Thompson Motors is a used car dealer that ------- in classic cars in excellent condition.

(A) restores 動 〜を修復する   (B) specializes 動 専門にする
(C) utilizes 動 利用する   (D) recommends 動 推薦する

(→ p. 36、**059**)

065. (D)

Because the delays at the factory persisted, clients were ------- the option of canceling their orders.

(A) selected 動 選んだ   (B) chosen 動 選んだ
(C) preferred 動 〜を好んだ   (D) given 動 〜を与えられた

(→ p. 38、**062**)

070. (B)

The customer satisfaction surveys ------- numerous ways in which the company can improve its service.

(A) extended 動 拡張した、伝えた   (B) revealed 動 明らかにした
(C) inquired 動 尋ねた   (D) prompted 動 促した

(→ p. 40、**069**)

075. (C)

Please be sure to be aboard the train by 1:00 P.M. as it will leave ------- thereafter.

(A) possibly 副 おそらく   (B) slowly 副 ゆっくり
(C) shortly 副 まもなく   (D) timely 副 タイムリーに

(→ p. 42、**071**)

080. (D)

The ------- candidate will be familiar with various types of social networking applications.

(A) spontaneous 形 自発的な   (B) hopeful 形 希望に満ちた
(C) constant 形 絶え間ない   (D) successful 形 成功した、うまくいく

(→ p. 44、**079**)

085. (A)

Ms. Briton was given an award for her ------- contribution to the museum's fundraising initiative.

(A) outstanding　形 ずば抜けた　　　　(B) trivial　形 さいな
(C) credential　形 信用の　　　　　　(D) humid　形 湿気の多い

(→ p. 46、**084**)

090. (B)

The advertising campaign for Nova Motors' new forklift will focus on the company's ------- for dependability.

(A) nomination　名 指名　　　　　　(B) reputation　名 評判
(C) identification　名 識別　　　　　(D) participation　名 参加

(→ p. 48、**089**)

095. (D)

The engineers at Giodani Constructions ------- a meticulous review of the bridge plans to ensure there would be no structural problems.

(A) committed　動 ～にかかわった　(B) registered　動 ～を登録した
(C) indicated　動 ～を指示した　　(D) conducted　動 ～を行った

(→ p. 50、**093**)

100. (C)

Denning Street in Central Morrisdale is one of the most ------- business addresses for accounting and legal firms.

(A) manageable　形 管理できる　　(B) durable　形 頑丈な
(C) desirable　形 好ましい　　　　(D) comparable　形 比較できる、同等な

(→ p. 52、**099**)

105. (A)

------- for the art director position must submit portfolios, which will be returned at the interview.

(A) Applicants　名 応募者たち　　(B) Recipients　名 受取人たち
(C) Advocates　名 支持者たち　　(D) Interns　名 インターンたち

(→ p. 54、**104**)

110. (D)

The factory ------- is aging, and it has become necessary to perform daily maintenance to ensure that it will run smoothly.

(A) workplace　名 職場　　　　　(B) mechanic　名 修理工
(C) technology　名 技術　　　　　(D) machinery　名 機械

(→ p. 56、**107**)

Unit 3
Set 1

111. To celebrate the special ------- , the Animus Concert Hall served complimentary drinks to everyone attending their first anniversary gala night.

112. The supervisor told Ms. Clarkson to order food in ------- to beverages for the upcoming company banquet.

113. The mayor raised the ------- that the new tunnel will not be finished in time for the city's anniversary celebrations.

114. Discount ------- is available for members of the Hamilton Art Gallery Association.

(A) addition
(B) occasion
(C) possibility
(D) admission

111. Ⓐ Ⓑ Ⓒ Ⓓ
112. Ⓐ Ⓑ Ⓒ Ⓓ
113. Ⓐ Ⓑ Ⓒ Ⓓ
114. Ⓐ Ⓑ Ⓒ Ⓓ

名詞07

選択肢

(A) addition 名 追加

(B) occasion 名 機会

(C) possibility 名 可能性

(D) admission 名 入場、入会金

正解・訳

111. (B)
特別な機会を祝うために、Animus Concert Hall は初めての記念特別興業の夕べの参加者全員に無料の飲み物を提供した。
complimentary: 無料の

112. (A)
上司は来る会社のパーティーのために、飲み物に追加して料理も注文するよう Clarkson さんに伝えた。
banquet: 宴会、パーティー

113. (C)
市長は新しいトンネルの完成が、市の記念日の祝典に間に合わない可能性を提起した。

114. (D)
Hamilton Art Gallery 協会の会員は入場料の割引を利用できる。

解説

111 (B) occasion は、よく special と一緒に「特別な日、機会」という意味で使われる。**112** は空所前後で in addition to ~（〜に加えて）に気付くことができると良い。**114** は、discount（割引の、割引価格の）とあるので料金に関する単語 (D) admission を選ぼう。

もう1問！

115. To ------- the special occasion, the Animus Concert Hall served complimentary drinks to everyone attending their first anniversary gala night.

   (A) commence (B) celebrate (C) certify (D) credit

▶▶▶ 解答は081ページ

Unit 3
Set 2

116. Please make sure to ------- all your belongings from the rental vehicle when you return it.

117. According to the itinerary, our flight will ------- at 7 A.M.

118. Thunder Coms Solutions will ------- from New York to Oregon in order to reduce its operating costs.

119. Buses are used to ------- passengers between the international and domestic terminals at Millhouse Airport.

(A) relocate
(B) remove
(C) transport
(D) depart

116. Ⓐ Ⓑ Ⓒ Ⓓ
117. Ⓐ Ⓑ Ⓒ Ⓓ
118. Ⓐ Ⓑ Ⓒ Ⓓ
119. Ⓐ Ⓑ Ⓒ Ⓓ

動詞07

選択肢

(A) relocate 動 移転する　　(B) remove 動 ～を取り去る、～を片付ける
(C) transport 動 ～を輸送する　(D) depart 動 出発する

正解・訳

116. (B)
レンタカーを返却する際には、確実に全ての荷物を降ろしてください。
make sure to ~: 確実に～する

117. (D)
旅程表によると、私たちの飛行機の便は午前7時に出発する。
itinerary: 旅程表

118. (A)
Thunder Coms Solutions は営業経費を削減するために New York から Oregon に移転する。

119. (C)
Millhouse 空港の国際線ターミナルと国内線ターミナル間の乗客を輸送するには、バスが使われている。
domestic: 国内の

解説

116の remove all your belongings は「確実に全ての荷物を取り除く」＝「お忘れ物がないように」という電車のアナウンスでもおなじみ。**118**の空所後にある from A to B という前置詞と共に用いられて目的語を必要としない動詞は relocate だ。**119**には空所後に目的語があるので、他動詞の(c)transport を選ぶ。

もう1問！

120. Buses are used to transport passengers between the international and ------- terminals at Millhouse Airport.

(A) internal　(B) in-house　(C) inside　(D) domestic

▶▶▶ 解答は081ページ

Unit 3
Set 3

121. To process the order, the name written on the form needs to be ------- to the one on the credit card.

122. Shoppers who come to the store's annual sale will enjoy ------- savings in all departments.

123. Renowned florist Gloria Wu is famous for her ------- taste and color coordination.

124. Customers have complained that the procedure for filling the printer with ink is too ------- .

(A) significant
(B) elaborate
(C) exquisite
(D) identical

121. Ⓐ Ⓑ Ⓒ Ⓓ
122. Ⓐ Ⓑ Ⓒ Ⓓ
123. Ⓐ Ⓑ Ⓒ Ⓓ
124. Ⓐ Ⓑ Ⓒ Ⓓ

形容詞05

選択肢

(A) significant 形 相当な
(B) elaborate 形 手の込んだ、複雑な
(C) exquisite 形 （感覚が）鋭い、洗練された
(D) identical 形 全く同じ、一致する

正解・訳

121. (D)
注文を処理するためには、用紙に記入された名前とクレジットカード上の名前が一致しなければならない。

122. (A)
店の毎年恒例のセールに来る買い物客は、全ての売り場で相当な得をする。
saving: 買い得、節約

123. (C)
有名なフローリストであるGloria Wuは、洗練されたセンスと色の合わせ方で知られている。
taste: センス、美的感覚

124. (B)
顧客たちは、プリンターにインクを入れる手順があまりに複雑過ぎると苦情を言った。

解説

121は空所後にあるtoに着目しidentical to ~（〜と同一の）という表現に気付けば素早く解答できる。**122**のsignificant（相当の）は最頻出単語の1つだ。副詞の形significantly（かなり）と共に覚えたい。**123**はexquisite taste（洗練されたセンス）とすると有名なフローリストの説明として妥当。

もう1問！

125. ------- florist Gloria Wu is famous for her exquisite taste and color coordination.

    (A) Named (B) Noticed (C)Renowned (D) Succeeded

▶▶▶ 解答は081ページ

Unit 3
Set 4

126. Due to rising fuel costs, the popularity of sports cars has decreased ------- over the past three years.

127. Pomona Wilderness Park is ------- closed until the footpaths damaged by the storm are repaired.

128. The human resources director asked the new recruits to read the employee manual ------- before they start work.

129. The Coronation Theater closed ------- three years ago, and the building is due to be demolished in a couple of months.

(A) thoroughly
(B) permanently
(C) currently
(D) considerably

126. Ⓐ Ⓑ Ⓒ Ⓓ
127. Ⓐ Ⓑ Ⓒ Ⓓ
128. Ⓐ Ⓑ Ⓒ Ⓓ
129. Ⓐ Ⓑ Ⓒ Ⓓ

副詞05

選択肢

(A) thoroughly 副 徹底的に、全く (B) permanently 副 永久に、恒久的に

(C) currently 副 今のところ、現在 (D) considerably 副 かなりの、相当な

正解・訳

126. (D)

燃料費の値上がりにより、スポーツカーの人気は過去3年の間にかなり下がった。

127. (C)

Pomona Wilderness Park は現在、嵐で損傷した歩道の修理が終わるまで閉鎖中である。

128. (A)

人事部長は、就業前に従業員マニュアルを徹底的に読むように新入社員に要請した。

129. (B)

Coronation Theater は3年前に永久的に閉館し、その建物は数カ月以内に解体される予定である。

due: (ある時期に)〜する予定である

解説

程度や時間を表す副詞が並んでいる。(D)の considerably（かなり）は程度を表し、**126** の空所前の decreased のように増減を表す動詞と相性が良い。(C) currently は now とほぼ同義で、**127** のような現在形や、現在進行形の文で用いられる。**129** は後半の「解体される予定だ」という文脈から (B) を選び、closed permanently（永久に閉館した、廃業した）とする。

もう1問！

130. Due to ------- fuel costs, the popularity of sports cars has decreased considerably over the past three years.

(A) rising (B) frustrated (C) raising (D) optimal

▶▶▶ 解答は081ページ

Unit 3
Set 5

131. The order will be shipped ------- the warehouse as soon as payment is confirmed.

132. In order to be competitive with other manufacturers' products, the new frozen dessert should be priced ------- five and seven dollars.

133. Passengers must always be greeted with a smile ------- boarding the aircraft.

134. This gift certificate can be used ------- a haircut or treatment at any Leno Hair Salon.

(A) upon
(B) toward
(C) between
(D) from

131. Ⓐ Ⓑ Ⓒ Ⓓ
132. Ⓐ Ⓑ Ⓒ Ⓓ
133. Ⓐ Ⓑ Ⓒ Ⓓ
134. Ⓐ Ⓑ Ⓒ Ⓓ

選択肢

(A) upon 　前　～するとすぐに　　(B) toward 　前　～のために、～の方に

(C) between 　前　～の間に　　(D) from 　前　～から

正解・訳

131. (D)

支払いが確認され次第、注文品は倉庫<u>から</u>出荷される。

132. (C)

他の製造業者の製品に対して競争力を持つためには、新しいフローズンデザートは5ドルから7ドル<u>の間</u>の値段がつけられるべきである。

133. (A)

乗客は、飛行機に乗って<u>すぐに</u>常に笑顔で迎えられなければならない。

134. (B)

このギフト券は、Leno Hair Salonの全店舗でのヘアカットかトリートメント<u>に使える。</u>

解説

131 は起点を表す (D) from を入れ、be shipped from ~（～から出荷される）とすると文意が通る。**132** は between A and B の形を想起し、即答したい。(A) upon は on とほぼ同じ意味だがやや硬い表現。**133** では「～するとすぐ」という意味で用いられている。(B) toward の原義は「～の方に」で、**134** ではクーポンの使い道を表している。

もう1問！

135. Passengers must always be ------- with a smile upon boarding the aircraft.

　　(A) dispatched　(B) represented　(C) exceeded　(D) greeted

▶▶▶ 解答は081ページ

Unit 3
Set 6

136. During the busy period, any ------- for time off should be made at least a week in advance.

137. You can improve your company's reputation by asking customers to post ------- online.

138. Dynamico user ------- cover topics such as operating procedures as well as basic maintenance.

139. Before ordering, please ensure that the product is suitable for your needs by checking the ------- listed in the catalog.

(A) testirnonials
(B) specifications
(C) manuals
(D) requests

136. Ⓐ Ⓑ Ⓒ Ⓓ
137. Ⓐ Ⓑ Ⓒ Ⓓ
138. Ⓐ Ⓑ Ⓒ Ⓓ
139. Ⓐ Ⓑ Ⓒ Ⓓ

名詞08

選択肢

(A) testimonials 名 お客様の声、証拠 (B) specifications 名 仕様、明細
(C) manuals 名 取扱説明書 (D) requests 名 依頼、要求

正解・訳

136. (D)
繁忙期の間は、いかなる休暇申請も最低でも1週間前には行うべきだ。

137. (A)
オンラインでお客様の声を投稿してもらうことで、会社の評判を向上させることができる。

138. (C)
Dynamico製品の取扱説明書には操作手順や基本のメンテナンス方法が記載されている。

139. (B)
ご注文前にカタログに記載されている製品の仕様をご確認いただき、ご要望に合うかを必ずご確認ください。

解説

(A) testimonialsには「証拠、証明書、推薦状」といった意味があるが、**137**のようにしばしば「お客様の声」の意味で出題される。動詞はtestify (証言する、証明する)。似た名詞にtestimony「(法廷で行う) 証言」があるが、平和なTOEICの世界では法廷に関するトピックはほぼ出題されないので、testimonialを覚えておこう。

もう1問！

140. Before ordering, please ensure that the product is ------- for your needs by checking the specifications listed in the catalog.

(A) available (B) suitable (C) reliable (D) enjoyable

▶▶▶ 解答は082ページ

Unit 3

Set 7

141. The two companies ------- the terms of their merger to the satisfaction of both groups of shareholders.

142. Having your vehicle serviced by anyone other than the ------- dealer may void your warranty.

143. Margaret Day is a very ------- musician with experience in a number of orchestras around the world.

144. The quarterly financial report will be ------- in an employee memo after the accounts department completes its review.

(A) authorized
(B) finalized
(C) accomplished
(D) summarized

141. Ⓐ Ⓑ Ⓒ Ⓓ
142. Ⓐ Ⓑ Ⓒ Ⓓ
143. Ⓐ Ⓑ Ⓒ Ⓓ
144. Ⓐ Ⓑ Ⓒ Ⓓ

動詞08

選択肢

(A) authorized 形 公認の 動 認可した、認可された

(B) finalized 動 最終決定した、最終決定された

(C) accomplished 形 一流の、熟練した 動 達成した、完成させた

(D) summarized 動 要約した、要約された

正解・訳

141. (B)

2つの会社は、双方の株主たちが満足する形で合併条件を<u>最終決定した</u>。

142. (A)

<u>正規販売店</u>以外で車両の点検整備を受けると、保証が無効になる場合があります。

void: ～を無効にする／warranty: 保証

143. (C)

Margaret Dayは、世界中の数あるオーケストラでの経験がある、とても<u>熟練した</u>ミュージシャンである。

144. (D)

四半期営業報告書は、経理部が審査した後、社内文書に<u>まとめられる</u>。

解説

選択肢には過去分詞-edが並んでおり、**141**と**144**では受動態の動詞の一部として、**142**と**143**では形容詞として使われている。(C) accomplished（達成した、熟練した、スキルの高い）は**143**のaccomplished musicianのように優れた音楽家や芸術家、実業家などを形容して使われるTOEIC頻出語だ。

もう1問！

145. Having your vehicle ------- by anyone other than the authorized dealer may void your warranty.

(A) awaited (B) automated (C) reviewed (D) serviced

Unit 3
Set 8

146. Mr. Martin's ------- report on the data from the online customer survey suggested that the recent changes had paid off.

147. Mr. Lu's extensive knowledge of both marketing and customer service make him a very ------- member of the team.

148. Although the teamwork seminar at IB Networks is ------- , most employees choose to attend.

149. During the busy period, Hanoi Delivery Services will hire employees on ------- contracts in order to reduce staffing costs.

    (A) temporary
    (B) preliminary
    (C) versatile
    (D) optional

146. Ⓐ Ⓑ Ⓒ Ⓓ
147. Ⓐ Ⓑ Ⓒ Ⓓ
148. Ⓐ Ⓑ Ⓒ Ⓓ
149. Ⓐ Ⓑ Ⓒ Ⓓ

形容詞06

選択肢

(A) temporary 形 臨時の、一時の　(B) preliminary 形 予備的な、準備のための
(C) versatile 形 多才な、何でもこなす (D) optional 形 任意の、自由選択の

正解・訳

146. (B)

オンライン顧客調査のデータについてのMartinさんの予備的な報告書は、最近の変革が功を奏したことを示唆している。
pay off: 成果を上げる

147. (C)

マーケティングと顧客サービスの両方の分野での幅広い知識があるため、Luさんはチームの中で、何でもこなすことができるメンバーである。

148. (D)

IB Networksでのチームワークに関するセミナーへの参加は任意であるにもかかわらず、ほとんどの社員が参加することを選ぶ。

149. (A)

Hanoi Delivery Servicesは、人件費を節約するために繁忙期には臨時契約で従業員を雇う。

解説

146は(B) を入れてpreliminary reportとすると「予備的な報告書」、すなわち「仮の報告書、中間報告書」となる。**147**は主語＋make＋人 ~(＜人＞を~にする) という形。(C) versatile (何でもこなす) は複数分野の知識を持つMr. Luを修飾する語としてふさわしい。**148**は文頭のAlthough (~にもかかわらず) に注目し、文意から(D) optional (任意の) を選ぶ。

もう1問！

150. Mr. Martin's preliminary report on the data from the online customer survey suggested that the recent changes had ------- off.

(A) put (B) took (C) came (D) paid

▶▶▶ 解答は082ページ

Unit 3
Set 9

151. To remain popular, mobile phone companies have to ------- develop their technology services or lose market share.

152. Analysts found that Markwell Pet Supplies had spent too ------- on marketing and too little on product development.

153. If you are ------- in Greenburg, you should make time to visit the Lundgren Art Gallery.

154. When organizing a charity dinner, make sure to send invitations early ------- so that the recipients can reply in time.

(A) ever
(B) much
(C) enough
(D) further

151. Ⓐ Ⓑ Ⓒ Ⓓ
152. Ⓐ Ⓑ Ⓒ Ⓓ
153. Ⓐ Ⓑ Ⓒ Ⓓ
154. Ⓐ Ⓑ Ⓒ Ⓓ

選択肢

(A) ever 副 いつか、一度でも　　(B) much 副 とても　形 たくさんの
(C) enough 副 十分に　形 十分な
(D) further 副 それ以上に　形 それ以上の

正解・訳

151. (D)

人気を保つために、携帯電話会社は技術サービスをさらに向上しなければ、市場シェアを失うことになる。

152. (B)

アナリストはMarkwell Pet Suppliesがマーケティングにあまりにも多くの金を使い、商品開発に金をかけなさ過ぎたことに気付いた。

153. (A)

もしGreenburgにいつか行くことがあれば、Lundgren Art Galleryを訪れる時間を取るべきだ。

154. (C)

慈善夕食会を企画する際は、受け取った人が期限内に返信できるよう、必ず十分に前もって招待状を送付してください。

解説

選択肢は副詞と、副詞にもなる形容詞。152のtoo（〜過ぎる）に続けられるのは、(C) muchのみ。空所後のtoo littleとも対になる。153のif you are ever inのeverはif（もし）を強調し、「もしいつか〜に行くことがあれば」という意味を添える。

もう1問！

155. When ------- a charity dinner, make sure to send invitations early
enough so that the recipients can reply in time.

(A) attending (B) allowing (C) organizing (D) obsessing

▶▶▶ 解答は082ページ

Unit 3
Set 10

156. The members of the marketing team ------- some time off after working so hard on the product launch.

157. Special training must be provided for employees before they ------- in specialized work.

158. KT Airline has agreed to ------- all passengers with tickets for flights canceled on account of the weather.

159. To help ------- traffic congestion during the festival, city officials are providing additional bus services.

(A) deserve
(B) relieve
(C) compensate
(D) engage

156. Ⓐ Ⓑ Ⓒ Ⓓ
157. Ⓐ Ⓑ Ⓒ Ⓓ
158. Ⓐ Ⓑ Ⓒ Ⓓ
159. Ⓐ Ⓑ Ⓒ Ⓓ

選択肢

(A) deserve 　動 ～を受けるに値する　　(B) relieve 　動 ～を軽減する、緩和する

(C) compensate 　動 ～に補償する、埋め合わせする

(D) engage 　動 従事する

正解・訳

156. (A)

マーケティングチームのメンバーは、商品発売の大仕事を終えたので、休暇を取るに値する。

launch: 立ち上げ、発売

157. (D)

専門職に従事する前に、従業員たちには特別な訓練が提供されるべきだ。

158. (C)

KT Airline は、天候の事情でキャンセルになったフライトのチケットを持った乗客全員に補償をすることに同意した。

on account of ~: ～の理由で

159. (B)

祭りの間の交通渋滞を緩和するため、市の職員たちはバスを増便している。

解説

157 は空所直後に注目。engage in ~ で「～に従事する、携わる」の意になる。158 は (C) compensate を入れて compensate all passengers（全乗客に補償をする）とする。158 のように、TOEIC ではよく inclement weather（悪天候）で飛行機が欠航する。

もう１問！

160. To help relieve traffic ------- during the festival, city officials are providing additional bus services.

(A) congestion　(B) renovation　(C) construction　(D) disruption

▶ ▶ ▶ 解答は082ページ

Unit 3
Set 11

161. Pauline Randall was excited to receive the community leadership award ------- for her work at the annual festival.

162. Ms. Harper's ------- to the town beautification campaign was highly valued by everyone involved.

163. You can get a ------- to *Imagine Aviation Magazine* on a quarterly, half-yearly or annual basis.

164. Advertisements that appear during *Weekly Roundup* do not necessarily imply the ------- of the program's producers.

   (A) subscription
   (B) nomination
   (C) endorsement
   (D) contribution

161. Ⓐ Ⓑ Ⓒ Ⓓ
162. Ⓐ Ⓑ Ⓒ Ⓓ
163. Ⓐ Ⓑ Ⓒ Ⓓ
164. Ⓐ Ⓑ Ⓒ Ⓓ

名詞09

選択肢

(A) subscription 名 (定期) 購読、会費 (B) nomination 名 推薦、候補者

(C) endorsement 名 承認、推薦 (D) contribution 名 貢献、寄付

正解・訳

161. (B)

Pauline Randall は、年に1度の祭りにおける仕事ぶりが評価され、地域社会のリーダーシップ賞への推薦を受けたことをとても喜んだ。

162. (D)

Harper さんの街の美化活動への貢献は、参加した全ての人から高く評価された。

163. (A)

Imagine Aviation Magazine は、3カ月間、半年間、もしくは、年間の定期購読が可能です。

164. (C)

Weekly Roundup 放送中に現れる広告は、必ずしもこの番組のプロデューサーたちの推薦を意味しない。

解説

163 の (A) subscription (定期購読) は頻出語で、Part 7にも雑誌や新聞の定期購読案内がよく出題される。更新すると購読料の割引やおまけなどの特典が受けられるパターンが多い。(C) endorsement は **164** では著名人による商品・サービスなどの「推奨、お墨付き」という意味で使われている。

もう1問！

165. Advertisements that appear during *Weekly Roundup* do not ------
imply the endorsement of the program's producers.

(A) actively (B) probably (C) necessarily (D) practically

▶▶▶ 解答は082ページ

Unit 3 もう1問！ 解答一覧

※問題文の訳は(→　　)内のページ・番号を参照してください

115. (B)

To ------- the special occasion, the Animus Concert Hall served complimentary drinks to everyone attending their first anniversary gala night.

(A) commence 動 ～を開始する (B) celebrate 動 ～を祝う
(C) certify 動 ～を証明する (D) credit 動 ～を認める

(→ p. 60、**111**)

120. (D)

Buses are used to transport passengers between the international and ------- terminals at Millhouse Airport.

(A) internal 形 内部の (B) in-house 形 社内の
(C) inside 形 内部の、秘密の (D) domestic 形 国内の

(→ p. 62、**119**)

125. (C)

------- florist Gloria Wu is famous for her exquisite taste and color coordination.

(A) Named 形 名付けられた (B) Noticed 形 気付かれた
(C) Renowned 形 有名な (D) Succeeded 動 ～の後に続いた

(→ p. 64、**123**)

130. (A)

Due to ------- fuel costs, the popularity of sports cars has decreased considerably over the past three years.

(A) rising 形 上昇しつつある (B) frustrated 形 いらいらした
(C) raising 動 上げている、募っている (D) optimal 形 最適な

(→ p. 66、**126**)

135. (D)

Passengers must always be ------- with a smile upon boarding the aircraft.

(A) dispatched 動 発送した、派遣した (B) represented 動 代表した
(C) exceeded 動 超過した (D) greeted 動 迎えた

(→ p. 68、**133**)

140. (B)

Before ordering, please ensure that the product is ------- for your needs by checking the specifications listed in the catalog.

(A) available 　形 利用できる
(B) suitable 　形 ふさわしい
(C) reliable 　形 信頼性のある
(D) enjoyable 　形 楽しい

(→ p. 70、**139**)

145. (D)

Having your vehicle ------- by anyone other than the authorized dealer may void your warranty.

(A) awaited 　動 待たれた
(B) automated 　動 自動化された
(C) reviewed 　動 評価された
(D) serviced 　動 修理された、整備された

(→ p. 72、**142**)

150. (D)

Mr. Martin's preliminary report on the data from the online customer survey suggested that the recent changes had ------- off.

(A) put 　動 置いた
(B) took 　動 取った
(C) came 　動 来た
(D) paid 　動 報われた

(→ p. 74、**146**)

155. (C)

When ------- a charity dinner, make sure to send invitations early enough so that the recipients can reply in time.

(A) attending 　動 ～に参加する
(B) allowing 　動 ～を許す
(C) organizing 　動 ～を企画する
(D) obsessing 　動 ～に取り付く

(→ p. 76、**154**)

160. (A)

To help relieve traffic ------- during the festival, city officials are providing additional bus services.

(A) congestion 　名 混雑
(B) renovation 　名 更新
(C) construction 　名 建設
(D) disruption 　名 混乱、中断

(→ p. 78、**159**)

165. (C)

Advertisements that appear during Weekly Roundup do not ------- imply the endorsement of the program's producers.

(A) actively 　副 積極的に
(B) probably 　副 多分
(C) necessarily 　副 必ずしも
(D) practically 　副 実質的に

(→ p. 80、**164**)

Unit 4
Set 1

166. To request an extension of sick leave, you need the ------- of a medical professional.

167. It is the employer's ------- to ensure the safety of the workplace.

168. If you have questions for a specific person, please refer to the ------- posted on the notice board and dial the appropriate extension.

169. A detailed ------- of your excursion is included, along with hotel information and maps.

(A) directory
(B) signature
(C) itinerary
(D) duty

166. (A) (B) (C) (D)
167. (A) (B) (C) (D)
168. (A) (B) (C) (D)
169. (A) (B) (C) (D)

名詞10

選択肢

(A) directory 名 名簿、電話帳　　(B) signature 名 署名、サイン

(C) itinerary 名 旅程表、旅行プラン　(D) duty 名 義務、任務、関税

正解・訳

166. (B)

病気休暇の延長を申請するには、医療専門家の署名が必要である。

167. (D)

職場の安全を確保するのは雇用主の義務である。

168. (A)

特定の人に質問がある場合は、掲示板の名簿を参照して、該当する内線番号に電話をおかけください。

appropriate: 適した、該当する

169. (C)

ご旅行の詳しい旅程表が、ホテルの情報と地図と一緒に同封されています。

excursion:小旅行

解説

(A)のdirectoryとは、名前や電話番号、住所などの情報が記載された名簿のこと。a company directory（社員名簿）、a telephone directory（電話帳）などの形で出る。(C)のitineraryは旅行の行動予定、移動手段、宿泊先などが一覧できる表のことで、Part 7にも頻出する。

もう1問！

170. A detailed itinerary of your ------- is included, along with hotel information and maps.

(A) expenditure　(B) experience　(C) excursion　(D) exception

▶▶▶ 解答は105ページ

Unit 4
Set 2

171. Despite the busy schedule, the members of Ms. Hill's team always ------- to submit their reports on time.

172. The budget surplus will ------- us to hold a company banquet to celebrate our success.

173. To ------- window displays for the upcoming holiday season, the staff at Redshine Department Store is working overtime.

174. To ------- the proper function of your new refrigerator, please consult the operation manual.

(A) prepare
(B) manage
(C) allow
(D) ensure

171. Ⓐ Ⓑ Ⓒ Ⓓ
172. Ⓐ Ⓑ Ⓒ Ⓓ
173. Ⓐ Ⓑ Ⓒ Ⓓ
174. Ⓐ Ⓑ Ⓒ Ⓓ

選択肢

(A) prepare [動] 〜を準備する

(B) manage [動] 〜に対処する、どうにか〜する

(C) allow [動] 〜を可能にする   (D) ensure [動] 〜を確実にする、請け合う

正解・訳

171. (B)

多忙なスケジュールにもかかわらず、Hillさんのチームのメンバーは、いつも期日までに報告書をどうにか提出する。

172. (C)

この予算の余りで、成功を祝うための会社の宴会を開くことができる。

surplus: 余り、余剰

173. (A)

来る休暇シーズン用のウインドー装飾を準備するため、Redshine Department Storeの従業員は残業をしている。

174. (D)

ご購入の新しい冷蔵庫が確実に正しく機能するように、操作マニュアルをご覧ください。

consult: 〜を調べる、閲覧する

解説

172は空所直後のusとto不定詞がヒント。allow 人 to doで「<人>が〜することを許す、〜できるようにする」の意になる。この文のように、TOEICの問題文に出てくる企業はよくbanquet(宴会、祝宴)を開く。新人歓迎会や退職者のお別れ会も多い。

もう1問！

175. To ensure the proper function of your new refrigerator, please ------- the operation manual.

(A) refer (B)complete (C) consult (D) classify

▶▶▶ 解答は105ページ

Unit 4

Set 3

176. The success of Freemont's agricultural industry should have positive ------- effects on other businesses in the town.

177. WorldWind Tours offers many ------- vacation packages for travelers on a budget.

178. Although Goldberg business machines are ------- to buy, they cost less to run.

179. Since she started work here in May, Ms. Dole has been a most ------- member of the sales team.

(A) affordable
(B) valuable
(C) expensive
(D) economic

176. Ⓐ Ⓑ Ⓒ Ⓓ
177. Ⓐ Ⓑ Ⓒ Ⓓ
178. Ⓐ Ⓑ Ⓒ Ⓓ
179. Ⓐ Ⓑ Ⓒ Ⓓ

形容詞07

選択肢

(A) affordable 形 手ごろな、良心的な価格の　　(B) valuable 形 貴重な、重要な

(C) expensive 形 費用のかかる、高価な　　(D) economic 形 経済の

正解・訳

176. (D)

Freemontの農産業の成功は、町の他のビジネスにも良い<u>経済</u>効果をもたらすだろう。

177. (A)

WorldWind Toursは、予算が限られた旅行客に、<u>手ごろな価格の</u>さまざまな休暇用パッケージツアーを提供している。

on a budget: 予算が限られた、予算通りの額で

178. (C)

Goldbergの事務機器は、買うには<u>費用がかかる</u>が、運用費は安い。

179. (B)

5月にここで働き始めてから、Doleさんは常に販売チームのとても<u>重要</u>なメンバーである。

解説

価値や価格に関する形容詞が並んでいる。**177**は、文の最後のon a budget（予算が限られた）から(A) affordableが正解。同意語にreasonable（手ごろな、妥当な）がある。**179**では、memberを形容できるのは(B) valuableのみだ。(C)は反意語のinexpensive（安価な）も覚えておこう。

もう1問！

180. WorldWind Tours offers many affordable vacation ------- for travelers on a budget.

(A) packages　(B) recipes　(C) packs　(D) policies

▶▶▶ 解答は105ページ

Unit 4

Set 4

181. Millions watched the game, which was broadcast ------- on television and the Internet.

182. When assigning parking spaces, administration staff choose employee names ------- to ensure fairness.

183. Production at the factory has been paused ------- as the cause of the product defects has not been identified.

184. Experts recommend getting to know your coworkers on a personal level as it can be ------- beneficial.

(A) indefinitely
(B) mutually
(C) randomly
(D) simultaneously

181. Ⓐ Ⓑ Ⓒ Ⓓ
182. Ⓐ Ⓑ Ⓒ Ⓓ
183. Ⓐ Ⓑ Ⓒ Ⓓ
184. Ⓐ Ⓑ Ⓒ Ⓓ

選択肢

(A) indefinitely 副 無期限に (B) mutually 副 互いに、相互に

(C) randomly 副 無作為に、無造作に (D) simultaneously 副 同時に

正解・訳

181. (D)

何百万もの人が、テレビとインターネットで同時に放送された試合を見た。

182. (C)

駐車場を割り当てる際、管理スタッフは公平を期すため従業員の名前を無作為に選ぶ。

183. (A)

製品の欠陥の原因が特定されていないので、その工場での生産は無期限に休止されている。

defect: 欠陥

184. (B)

専門家たちは、互いに有益になり得るので、同僚を個人的に知ることを推奨している。

解説

182は to ensure fairness（公平を期すために）から、抽選が「無作為に、ランダムに」行われたと考えるのが妥当。(A) indefinitely は definite（明確に区切られた）に「不、無」を意味する接頭辞 in と副詞の語尾 ly が添えられていることから「無期限に」という意味になる。

もう1問！

185. Production at the factory has been ------- indefinitely as the cause of the product defects has not been identified.

(A) resumed (B) deleted (C) redeemed (D) paused

▶▶▶ 解答は105ページ

Unit 4
Set 5

186. Incident reports should be filled out immediately, ------- to satisfy company requirements.

187. According to the audience members at her presentation, Ms. Lee spoke French ------- she had lived in France all her life.

188. Evens Pharmaceuticals plans to spend more money on research ------- none of its current projects has produced any useful results.

189. Many more people have started using portable electronic devices ------- they have become more affordable.

   (A) even though
   (B) if only
   (C) as though
   (D) now that

186. Ⓐ Ⓑ Ⓒ Ⓓ
187. Ⓐ Ⓑ Ⓒ Ⓓ
188. Ⓐ Ⓑ Ⓒ Ⓓ
189. Ⓐ Ⓑ Ⓒ Ⓓ

接続詞02

選択肢

(A) even though　〜にもかかわらず
(B) if only　ただ〜でさえあればいいのだが、(to〜で)〜するためにも
(C) as though　まるで〜であるかのように　(D) now that　今や〜なので

正解・訳

186. (B)

事故報告書は、企業の要件を満たす<u>ためにも</u>、直ちに記入されるべきである。

187. (C)

彼女のプレゼンテーションの聴衆によると、Leeさんは<u>まるで</u>ずっとフランス暮らし<u>であるかのように</u>フランス語を話したそうだ。

188. (A)

Evens Pharmaceuticalsは、最近のプロジェクトのどれもが有益な結果を出していない<u>にもかかわらず</u>、研究にさらに資金を投じることを計画している。

189. (D)

<u>今や</u>手ごろな価格になった<u>ので</u>、より多くの人が携帯電子機器を使い始めている。

解説

186は空所直後のtoがヒント。接続詞(句)の後には基本的に節(主語＋動詞)が続くが、if onlyはto不定詞を伴い「〜するためにも」という意味になる。**188**では、「さらに資金を投じる」と「どのプロジェクトも利益を出していない」をつなぐには、譲歩を表す(A) even thoughが適切。

もう1問！

190. Many more people have started using ------- electronic devices now that they have become more affordable.

(A) handful　(B) portable　(C) skillful　(D) moving

▶▶▶ 解答は105ページ

Unit 4

Set 6

191. After the supervisor's introduction had concluded, attendees were encouraged to ask questions that were ------- to the discussion.

192. To stay up-to-date with the latest news and ------- events in Oaksville, please register with the town's e-mail newsletter.

193. A ------- schedule was created when organizers learned that one of the conference speakers would arrive late.

194. Some ------- tables and chairs were set up on the restaurant's balcony when a group arrived without a reservation.

(A) revised
(B) additional
(C) current
(D) relevant

191. Ⓐ Ⓑ Ⓒ Ⓓ
192. Ⓐ Ⓑ Ⓒ Ⓓ
193. Ⓐ Ⓑ Ⓒ Ⓓ
194. Ⓐ Ⓑ Ⓒ Ⓓ

選択肢

(A) revised 〔形〕改訂された、修正された　(B) additional 〔形〕追加の

(C) current 〔形〕現在の　　　　　　　　　(D) relevant 〔形〕関連した

正解・訳

191. (D)

監督者の導入が終わった後、出席者たちはその議論に<u>関連した</u>質問をするよう勧められた。

192. (C)

Oaksvilleの最新ニュースと<u>現在の</u>出来事を常に把握するために、町のメールニュースレターに登録してください。

193. (A)

主催者が会議の講演者の1人が遅れると知った時、<u>改訂版の</u>スケジュールが作られた。

194. (B)

予約なしの団体客が来たので、レストランのバルコニーに<u>追加の</u>テーブルと椅子が用意された。

解説

191の(D) relevant to ~は、related to（~に関連した）とも言い換えられる。**193**の(B) additionalは再頻出の語。動詞add（加える）、名詞addition（追加）、副詞additionally（加えて）と並んで文法問題で問われる。in addition to ~（~に加えて）も覚えておこう。

もう1問！

195. After the supervisor's introduction had ------- , attendees were encouraged to ask questions that were relevant to the discussion.

(A) terminated (B) concluded (C) closed (D) exclaimed

▶▶▶ 解答は106ページ

Unit 4
Set 7

196. Mr. Gregory's team has been asked to ------- a software application to help warehouse employees keep track of inventory.

197. A monthly maintenance routine will ------- the life of your equipment and save you money in the long run.

198. Quadpoint Electronics decided not to ------- with the merger because it could not accept some of TPG Holdings' conditions.

199. Mr. Alton did not ------- on time for the first day of the medical conference because he had missed his flight.

(A) proceed
(B) arrive
(C) develop
(D) extend

196. Ⓐ Ⓑ Ⓒ Ⓓ
197. Ⓐ Ⓑ Ⓒ Ⓓ
198. Ⓐ Ⓑ Ⓒ Ⓓ
199. Ⓐ Ⓑ Ⓒ Ⓓ

選択肢

(A) proceed 動 始める、続行する、進む　　(B) arrive 動 到着する

(C) develop 動 ～を成長させる、開発する　(D) extend 動 ～を延ばす、示す

正解・訳

196. (C)

Gregoryさんのチームは、倉庫の従業員が在庫の記録をつけるのを助けるソフトウェアアプリの開発を依頼されている。

inventory: 在庫品、全商品の一覧表／keep track of ~: ～の経過を追う、～の記録をつける

197. (D)

毎月のメンテナンスのルーティンは、機器の寿命を<u>延ばす</u>ので、結局はお金の節約になる。

198. (A)

Quadpoint Electronicsは、TPG Holdingsの条件のいくつかを受け入れることができなかったので、合併を<u>進め</u>ないことを決めた。

199. (B)

Altonさんは飛行機に乗り遅れたため、医学学会の初日に時間通りに<u>到着</u>しなかった。

解説

198は空所直後のwithがヒント。自動詞の(A) proceedを入れて、proceed with ~（～を進める、始める）という形になる。**196**、**197**は空所直後に目的語があるので他動詞が入る。文意からそれぞれ(C) develop（～を開発する）、(D) extend（～を延ばす）が適当。

もう1問！

200. A monthly maintenance ------- will extend the life of your equipment and save you money in the long run.

(A) submission　(B) opportunity　(C) duration　(D) routine

▶▶▶ 解答は106ページ

Unit 4
Set 8

201. After working all day without a break, Ms. Sanders
------- couldn't concentrate in the meeting.

202. The company president asked that employees
contact her ------- with ideas to improve sales.

203. Peterson's Desserts is gradually building a
customer base in England and ------- hopes to
export desserts to other European countries.

204. Steel prices increased last month, and construction
costs are predicted to rise ------- in the coming
weeks.

(A) eventually
(B) accordingly
(C) directly
(D) simply

201. Ⓐ Ⓑ Ⓒ Ⓓ
202. Ⓐ Ⓑ Ⓒ Ⓓ
203. Ⓐ Ⓑ Ⓒ Ⓓ
204. Ⓐ Ⓑ Ⓒ Ⓓ

選択肢

(A) eventually 　副 最終的には、ゆくゆくは

(B) accordingly 　副 それに応じて、結果として

(C) directly 　副 直接　　(D) simply 　副 単純に、とにかく、どうしても

正解・訳

201. (D)

休みも取らずに1日中働いた後で、Sandersさんはどうしても会議に集中できなかった。

202. (C)

その会社の社長は、売り上げを伸ばすためのアイデアを直接知らせるよう従業員に頼んだ。

203. (A)

Peterson's Dessertsはイングランドで徐々に顧客基盤を築いており、ゆくゆくは他のヨーロッパ諸国にもデザートを輸出したいと考えている。

204. (B)

先月、鉄鋼の価格が上がったので、それに応じて今後数週間のうちに建設費用も上がるだろうと予想される。

解説

(A) eventuallyや(B) accordinglyといった副詞が選択肢に並んでいる場合は、問題文の時間の流れや前後の因果関係に注目しよう。**203**はイングランドからヨーロッパへ「ゆくゆくは」進出したいという流れが自然なのでeventually、**204**は先月の鉄鋼の価格上昇に応じて今後コストが上がるという文脈を見抜きaccordinglyを選ぼう。

もう1問！

205. Steel prices increased last month, and construction costs are predicted to ------- accordingly in the coming weeks.

(A) fall　(B) ease　(C) multiply　(D) rise

▶▶▶ 解答は106ページ

Unit 4
Set 9

206. Kitchen workers are required to be familiar with all government ------- related to food handling.

207. Freeman Associates often hires employees based on personal ------- from other staff members.

208. There are ------- that the construction project is not going smoothly as expected.

209. Event organizers must follow the ------- for the use of the equipment in the conference room.

(A) recommendations
(B) directions
(C) suggestions
(D) regulations

206. Ⓐ Ⓑ Ⓒ Ⓓ
207. Ⓐ Ⓑ Ⓒ Ⓓ
208. Ⓐ Ⓑ Ⓒ Ⓓ
209. Ⓐ Ⓑ Ⓒ Ⓓ

名詞11

選択肢

(A) recommendations 〔名〕推薦、推薦状　(B) directions 〔名〕説明（書）

(C) suggestions 〔名〕提案、～の兆候、気配

(D) regulations 〔名〕規制、規則

正解・訳

206. (D)

厨房で働く人は、食品取り扱いに関する全ての政府の<u>規制</u>を熟知している必要がある。

207. (A)

Freeman Associatesは、他の職員の個人的な<u>推薦状</u>によって従業員を雇うことがよくある。

208. (C)

その建設プロジェクトは予想されたように順調には進まない<u>気配</u>がある。

209. (B)

イベントの主催者たちは、会議室の機器を使用するのに、この<u>説明書</u>に従わなければならない。

解説

206のcomply with ~は「～に従う、応じる」。食品取り扱いにおいて知っておかなければいけないのは(D)のregulationsだ。(A)の recommendationsは可算名詞では「推薦状、特定のものの推薦」という意味。(C)のsuggestionsには「提案」の他、「～の兆候、気配」という意味もある。

もう1問！

210. Event organizers must ------- the directions for the use of the equipment in the conference room.

(A) keep (B) follow (C) ask (D) cover

▶▶▶ 解答は106ページ

Unit 4
Set 10

211. Starting in August, East Shores Corporation plans to ------- a new dress code policy for employees.

212. Mandel Paper Company has been contracted to ------- copy paper and other stationery to the local government offices.

213. In order to ------- the business's profitability, it may be necessary to diversify our product line.

214. Members of the local community are encouraged to ------- a few hours toward a cleanup campaign on Saturday, March 7.

(A) supply
(B) implement
(C) maintain
(D) contribute

211. Ⓐ Ⓑ Ⓒ Ⓓ
212. Ⓐ Ⓑ Ⓒ Ⓓ
213. Ⓐ Ⓑ Ⓒ Ⓓ
214. Ⓐ Ⓑ Ⓒ Ⓓ

動詞12

選択肢

(A) supply [動] 〜を供給する　(B) implement [動] 〜を実行する、実施する

(C) maintain [動] 〜を維持する、主張する

(D) contribute [動] 〜に貢献する、寄付する

正解・訳

211. (B)

8月から、East Shores Corporation は従業員に対して新しい服装規定の適用を実施する。

212. (A)

Mandel Paper Company は、地方自治体の事務所にコピー用紙やその他の文具を供給する契約を結んでいる。

213. (C)

事業の収益性を維持するために、わが社の製品ラインを多様化することが必要かもしれない。

profitability: 収益性

214. (D)

地域コミュニティーのメンバーは、3月7日・土曜日の清掃運動に数時間貢献するよう奨励されている。

解説

(A) supply は、**212** のように動詞「供給する」という意味でも、名詞「供給、必需品」という意味でも頻出語だ。オフィスで必要な備品を指す office supplies もよく出題されるので、併せて覚えておこう。この場合は複数形で使われる。

もう1問！

215. Mandel Paper Company has been ------- to supply copy paper and other stationery to the local government offices.

(A) affected　(B) conducted　(C) promoted　(D) contracted

▶▶▶ 解答は106ページ

Unit 4
Set 11

216. Place the crystal flower vases carefully in the box, and do not use ------- force.

217. The new FX10 truck has been made ------- enough to handle even the most demanding roads.

218. Over the years, doctors have continued to make ------- progress on improving health care for elderly patients.

219. Writers of ------- travel reports are required to include a summary when they submit them to management.

(A) considerable
(B) sturdy
(C) lengthy
(D) excessive

216. Ⓐ Ⓑ Ⓒ Ⓓ
217. Ⓐ Ⓑ Ⓒ Ⓓ
218. Ⓐ Ⓑ Ⓒ Ⓓ
219. Ⓐ Ⓑ Ⓒ Ⓓ

選択肢

(A) considerable [形] かなりの　　　　　　(B) sturdy [形] 頑丈な、丈夫な

(C) lengthy [形] 長期にわたる、冗長な　　(D) excessive [形] 過度の、過剰な

正解・訳

216. (D)

クリスタルの花瓶を注意して箱に入れ、また、<u>過度の</u>力をかけないでください。

217. (B)

この新しいFX10 トラックは、かなり過酷な道でも対処できるよう<u>頑丈</u>に作られている。

218. (A)

何年にもわたり医師たちは高齢患者対象の医療について<u>かなりの</u>前進を遂げてきた。

219. (C)

<u>長い</u>出張報告書を書いた者は、経営管理者にそれを提出する際に要約を付けることを求められている。

解説

(A) considerable は動詞 consider「考える」＋ able「〜できる」から「（考えられる範囲の）かなり」。一方、(D) excessive は「過度の、過剰な」とネガティブな意味合いがある。よって**218**は considerable progress「かなりの進歩」とするのが適切。progress にネガティブな修飾語は合わない。

もう1問！

220. The new FX10 truck has been made sturdy enough to handle even the most ------- roads.

(A) demanding (B) serious (C) critical (D) severe

▶▶▶ 解答は106ページ

Unit 4 もう1問！ 解答一覧

※問題文の訳は(→　)内のページ・番号を参照してください

170. (C)

A detailed itinerary of your ------- is included, along with hotel information and maps.

(A) expenditure　名 支出 (B) experience　名 経験
(C) excursion　名 旅行 (D) exception　名 例外

(→ p. 84、**169**)

175. (C)

To ensure the proper function of your new refrigerator, please ------- the operation manual.

(A) refer　動 (toを伴って)~を参照する (B) complete　動 完了する
(C) consult　動 閲覧する、参考にする (D) classify　動 分類する

(→ p. 86、**174**)

180. (A)

WorldWind Tours offers many affordable vacation ------- for travelers on a budget.

(A) packages　名 パッケージ、旅行 (B) recipes　名 レシピ
(C) packs　名 箱、集まり (D) policies　名 方針

(→ p. 88、**177**)

185. (D)

Production at the factory has been ------- indefinitely as the cause of the product defects has not been identified.

(A) resumed　動 再開した (B) deleted　動 削除された
(C) redeemed　動 換金された (D) paused　動 休止した

(→ p. 90、**183**)

190. (B)

Many more people have started using ------- electronic devices now that they have become more affordable.

(A) handful　形 一握りの (B) portable　形 携帯可能な
(C) skillful　形 熟練した、腕のいい (D) moving　形 移動する、感動的な

(→ p. 92、**189**)

195. (B)

After the supervisor's introduction had ------- , attendees were encouraged to ask questions that were relevant to the discussion.

(A) terminated 　[動] 終了した、解雇された　(B) concluded 　[動] (話や会議が) 終わった
(C) closed 　[動] 締めくくった　(D) exclaimed 　[動] 叫んだ

(→ p. 94、**191**)

200. (D)

A monthly maintenance ------- will extend the life of your equipment and save you money in the long run.

(A) submission 　[名] 提出　(B) opportunity 　[名] 機会
(C) duration 　[名] 期間　(D) routine 　[名] ルーティン

(→ p. 96、**197**)

205. (D)

Steel prices increased last month, and construction costs are predicted to ------- accordingly in the coming weeks.

(A) fall 　[動] 落ちる　(B) ease 　[動] 和らぐ
(C) multiply 　[動] 増加させる　(D) rise 　[動] 上昇する

(→ p. 98、**204**)

210. (B)

Event organizers must ------- the directions for the use of the equipment in the conference room.

(A) keep 　[動] ～を保つ　(B) follow 　[動] ～に従う
(C) ask 　[動] ～に頼む　(D) cover 　[動] ～を覆う、～を扱う

(→ p. 100、**209**)

215. (D)

Mandel Paper Company has been ------- to supply copy paper and other stationery to the local government offices.

(A) affected 　[動] 影響を及ぼした　(B) conducted 　[動] 実施した
(C) promoted 　[動] 推進した　(D) contracted 　[動] ～と契約した

(→ p. 102、**212**)

220. (A)

The new FX10 truck has been made sturdy enough to handle even the most ------- roads.

(A) demanding 　[形] 厳しい、過酷な　(B) serious 　[形] 深刻な
(C) critical 　[形] 危機的な　(D) severe 　[形] 厳密な、(天気などが) 厳しい

(→ p. 104、**217**)

Unit 5
Set 1

221. Organizers have received bids from Day's Catering and Dilbert Food Services, and they are likely to choose the ------- .

222. Sales staff are recommended to greet ------- customers individually to help encourage them to sign up.

223. If you require transportation services from the hotel to your conference location, we would appreciate ------- notice.

224. The environmentalists argue that we should make ------- changes to our lifestyles to help reduce carbon emissions.

(A) potential
(B) immediate
(C) prior
(D) former

221. Ⓐ Ⓑ Ⓒ Ⓓ
222. Ⓐ Ⓑ Ⓒ Ⓓ
223. Ⓐ Ⓑ Ⓒ Ⓓ
224. Ⓐ Ⓑ Ⓒ Ⓓ

形容詞10

選択肢

(A) potential 形 見込みがある、潜在的な

(B) immediate 形 即時の、緊急の、差し迫った

(C) prior 形 前の、事前の　(D) former 形 前の 名 (the~) 前者

正解・訳

221. (D)

主催者は Day's Catering と Dilbert Food Services から入札を受け、前者を選ぶようである。
bid: 入札

222. (A)

販売員たちは契約を促すために、見込み客の一人ひとりに挨拶するよう勧められている。

223. (C)

ホテルから会議が行われる場所までの移動手段が必要な場合は、事前にお知らせをいただけると幸いです。

224. (B)

環境保護主義者は、二酸化炭素排出を減らすために、われわれは即時に生活様式を変更するべきだと主張する。

解説

(C) prior、(D) former ともに「前の」という意味があるが、prior は「事前の、前もっての」、former は「かつての、元〜（役職）」。また the former は「（2つ挙げたうちの）前者」という意味。221 では2社の名前が挙げられているので、1つを選ぶ former が適切。「後者」は the latter。

もう1問！

225. Organizers have received ------- from Day's Catering and Dilbert Food Services, and they are likely to choose the former.

(A) bets　(B) statements　(C) bids　(D) billings

▶▶▶ 解答は129ページ

Unit 5

Set 2

226. Highway 86 has ------- congested traffic in the evenings and should be avoided when possible.

227. With more than 50 locations in Oregon alone, Dustin's is ------- one of the country's most popular carwashes.

228. The Sizemore City Council will replace ------- half of its buses with electric vehicles this year.

問題226～230 Unit 5

229. Despite his success in the United States, Freddie Coleman is ------- unknown in his home country of Scotland.

(A) roughly
(B) heavily
(C) clearly
(D) largely

226. Ⓐ Ⓑ Ⓒ Ⓓ
227. Ⓐ Ⓑ Ⓒ Ⓓ
228. Ⓐ Ⓑ Ⓒ Ⓓ
229. Ⓐ Ⓑ Ⓒ Ⓓ

副詞08

選択肢

(A) roughle 副 おおよそ   (B) heavily 副 大量に、非常に

(C) clearly 副 はっきりと、明瞭に   (D) largely 副 主に、大部分は

正解・訳

226. (B)

幹線道路86号は夕刻は非常に渋滞するので、可能な場合は避けた方がよい。

227. (C)

Oregonだけで50店舗もあり、Dustin'sは明らかに国内で最も人気のある洗車場の1つだ。

228. (A)

Sizemore市議会は今年、おおよそ半分のバスを電気自動車に切り替える。

229. (D)

Freddie Colemanは、アメリカでは成功しているにもかかわらず、故郷のスコットランドではほとんど知られていない。

解説

空所直後の語との相性で解く。**226**のcongested traffic（渋滞）と相性がいいのはheavily。**228**のhalfのように量や数を表す語の前は、roughly（おおよそ）やabout（約）などが合う。**229**はlargely unknownで「ほとんど不明の、知られていない」。

もう1問！

230. Highway 86 has heavily congested ------- in the evenings and should be avoided when possible.

(A) route (B) traffic (C) vehicle (D) pavement

▶▶▶ 解答は129ページ

Unit 5
Set 3

231. Merkam Bay has hired additional ------- to help clean the local beaches.

232. The ------- at the marketing seminar were excited to hear about Max Schumacher's latest advertising campaign.

233. *Film Now* is an industry journal that features articles on the latest video equipment and ------- of outstanding new filmmakers.

234. At the closing ceremony, Laguna Oaks Academy will recognize the three most outstanding ------- of the year with memorial plaques.

(A) attendees
(B) personnel
(C) profiles
(D) graduates

231. Ⓐ Ⓑ Ⓒ Ⓓ
232. Ⓐ Ⓑ Ⓒ Ⓓ
233. Ⓐ Ⓑ Ⓒ Ⓓ
234. Ⓐ Ⓑ Ⓒ Ⓓ

名詞12

選択肢

(A) attendees 名 出席者   (B) personnel 名 社員、人事部

(C) profiles 名 プロフィール、人物紹介   (D) graduates 名 卒業生

解答・訳

231. (B)

Merkam Bay は、その地域の海岸を清掃するために、追加の社員を雇った。

232. (A)

マーケティングセミナーの出席者は、Max Schumacher の最新の広告キャンペーンのことを聞いて興奮した。

233. (C)

Film Now は業界紙で、最新のビデオ機器と優れた新しい映画製作者の人物紹介の記事を呼び物にしている。

234. (D)

閉会式で、Laguna Oaks Academy は、その年の最も傑出した3人の卒業生を記念の盾で表彰するだろう。
plaque:（記念の）盾

解説

231 の personnel（社員）は最後の音節にアクセントがある。綴りのよく似た形容詞 personal（個人の）は最初の音節にアクセントがあるので、この機会に区別しておこう。**234** の outstanding（傑出した）も優れた人や業績を形容する語として TOEIC 頻出だ。

もう1問！

235. *Film Now* is an industry journal that ------- articles on the latest video equipment and profiles of outstanding new filmmakers.

    (A) validates (B) features (C) advocates (D) appears

▶▶▶ 解答は129ページ

Unit 5
Set 4

236. After you ------- in the craft class, make sure to buy all the required materials.

237. Ms. Reed's presentation will ------- some photographs and videos that are sure to impress the audience.

238. A technician will ------- some new booking software at Wenham Hotel today because of constant system errors.

239. The council will probably ------- a resolution on the budget at the next town hall meeting this Friday.

(A) install
(B) enroll
(C) adopt
(D) incorporate

236. Ⓐ Ⓑ Ⓒ Ⓓ
237. Ⓐ Ⓑ Ⓒ Ⓓ
238. Ⓐ Ⓑ Ⓒ Ⓓ
239. Ⓐ Ⓑ Ⓒ Ⓓ

動詞13

選択肢

(A) install 　動　～をインストールする、導入する

(B) enroll 　動　登録する、入会する

(C) adopt 　動　～を採択する　(D) incorporate 　動　～を取り入れる、組み込む

正解・訳

236. (B)

工芸クラスに入会したら、必ず全ての必要な材料を購入してください。

237. (D)

Reedさんのプレゼンテーションは、確実に聞き手に好印象を与える写真や動画を取り入れるだろう。

238. (A)

Wenham Hotelでは、システムエラーが続いているので、技術者が新しい予約管理ソフトウェアを今日インストールする。

239. (C)

議会はおそらく今週金曜日の町役会議で、予算における決議を採択するだろう。

解説

236はenroll in ~で「～に入る、入学する」。(A) install（～をインストールする）は**238**の「コンピューターにソフトウェアをインストールする」という意味の他に「設備、装置、家具などを取り付ける、設置する」という意味があり、どちらもよく出題される。

もう1問！

240. The council will probably adopt a ------- on the budget at the next town hall meeting this Friday.

(A) solution (B) method (C) resolution (D) rule

▶▶▶ 解答は129ページ

Unit 5

Set 5

241. The factory has invested in a filtration system ------- the local environment.

242. Many stores sold out of the Dishlux frying pan ------- the unexpectedly successful marketing campaign.

243. Please use this industrial vacuum cleaner ------- the instructions printed in the manual.

244. The firm's position ------- vacation days is stated in each employee's signed contract.

(A) in accordance with
(B) with regard to
(C) in consequence of
(D) for the sake of

241. Ⓐ Ⓑ Ⓒ Ⓓ
242. Ⓐ Ⓑ Ⓒ Ⓓ
243. Ⓐ Ⓑ Ⓒ Ⓓ
244. Ⓐ Ⓑ Ⓒ Ⓓ

選択肢

(A) in accordance with　～に従って　　(B) with regard to　～に関する

(C) in consequence of　～の結果として　(D) for the sake of　～のために

正解・訳

241. (D)

その工場は、地域の環境のために、ろ過作用浄水システムに投資した。

filtration system: ろ過作用浄水システム

242. (C)

販売キャンペーンが予想外にうまくいった<u>結果として</u>、たくさんの店でDishluxのフライパンが売り切れた。

243. (A)

この業務用掃除機をマニュアルに印刷された説明<u>に従って</u>使ってください。

244. (B)

休暇日数に<u>関する</u>会社側の見解は、それぞれの従業員がサインをした契約書に明記されている。

解説

(A) in accordance with ~ は「～（法律、規則、マニュアルの指示）に従って」。似た表現のaccording to ~「～によれば、～に従って」も覚えておこう。**242**は空所前の「フライパンが売り切れた」と空所後の「予想外に成功したキャンペーン」を因果関係にすることができる(C)が正解。

もう1問！

245. Many stores sold out of the Dishlux frying pan in consequence of the ------- successful marketing campaign.

　　(A) generously　(B) barely　(C) inefficiently　(D) unexpectedly

▶▶▶ 解答は129ページ

Unit 5

Set 6

246. Nileways Home Shopping will ------- the shipping costs for orders placed before June 10.

247. One way to ------- the manufacturing cost is to use less expensive materials.

248. Dream Flares' customers can ------- their frequent flyer miles on the airline's Web site.

249. Employees should ------- their old security badges as soon as they receive their new ones.

(A) waive
(B) reduce
(C) redeem
(D) discard

246. Ⓐ Ⓑ Ⓒ Ⓓ
247. Ⓐ Ⓑ Ⓒ Ⓓ
248. Ⓐ Ⓑ Ⓒ Ⓓ
249. Ⓐ Ⓑ Ⓒ Ⓓ

動詞14

選択肢

(A) waive 動 ~（権利や条件）を放棄する　　(B) reduce 動 ~を減らす

(C) redeem 動 ~を（商品と）引き換える

(D) discard 動 ~を捨てる、破棄する

正解・訳

246. (A)

Nileways Home Shoppingは、7月10日よりも前のご注文については送料を<u>いただきません</u>。

247. (B)

製造コストを<u>減らす</u>方法の1つは、より安い原料を使うことだ。

248. (C)

Dream Flaresの顧客は、同航空会社のウェブサイトでマイルを<u>交換</u>することができる。

frequent flyer miles: マイル ※マイレージサービスを受けるためのマイル数

249. (D)

従業員は新しい入館証を受け取り次第、古いものを<u>破棄</u>しなければならない。

解説

(D) discard（~を捨てる）は、物やデータなどを破棄する意味で出題されるが、discard a prejudice（偏見を捨てる）やdiscard old habits（古い習慣を捨てる）など目に見えないものにも使われる。最近、TOEICの世界でもペーパーレス化が進んでいるようで、discard old papers/documents（古い書類を廃棄する）という話もよく出てくる。

もう1問！

250. Employees should discard their old security ------- as soon as they receive their new ones.

(A) gates (B) vouchers (C) badges (D) features

Unit 5

Set 7

251. It is not ------- to expand the company until we resolve the labor shortage issue.

252. The Everland Construction Group is ------- of handling multiple building contracts at one time.

253. While Beaumont Kitchenware and Pots, Pans 'n' More sell ------- items, their prices are very different.

254. Ms. Ames will most ------- start work at Carleton Plumbing in March, as she needs to give her current employer two weeks' notice.

(A) similar
(B) likely
(C) feasible
(D) capable

251. Ⓐ Ⓑ Ⓒ Ⓓ
252. Ⓐ Ⓑ Ⓒ Ⓓ
253. Ⓐ Ⓑ Ⓒ Ⓓ
254. Ⓐ Ⓑ Ⓒ Ⓓ

形容詞11

選択肢

(A) similar [形] 類似の、同じような　　(B) likely [副] たぶん　[形] ～しそうだ

(C) feasible [形] 実現可能な　　(D) capable [形] 能力がある、有能な

正解・訳

251. (C)

人員不足の問題を解消するまで、会社の拡大は実現可能ではない。

252. (D)

Everland Construction Group は、同時に複数のビルの建設を担当することが可能である。

253. (A)

Beaumont Kitchenware と Pots, Pans 'n' More は類似した商品を販売しているが、値段にはかなりの差がある。

254. (B)

Ames さんは、現在の雇い主に退職の2週間前に退職通知を渡す必要があるので、おそらく3月から Carleton Plumbing で働くだろう。

解説

251 は (B) likely も入りそうに思えるが、これを空所に入れると「それは会社を拡大しそうにない」となり、「それ」が何を指すかが不明確になる。よって、(B) は不正解だ。(C) を入れれば冒頭の It は to expand the company（会社を拡大すること）を指す形式主語となり、文が成り立つ。

もう1問！

255. It is not feasible to expand the company until we ------- the labor shortage issue.

　　　(A) resolve (B) postpone (C) intrigue (D) concentrate

▶▶▶ 解答は130ページ

Unit 5

Set 8

256. Over the past three years, McMillan Frozen Dinners has ------- increased its market share from 5 percent to almost 20 percent.

257. The supervisor recommends that all agents ------- update their travel expense reports to avoid late payments.

258. Ms. Penkala is ------- free on Monday mornings, so that is the best time to arrange an appointment on Monday mornings.

問題256-260 Unit 5

259. The Private Holdings Bank will send you your personal identification number ------- your registration is complete.

(A) usually
(B) once
(C) regularly
(D) steadily

256. Ⓐ Ⓑ Ⓒ Ⓓ
257. Ⓐ Ⓑ Ⓒ Ⓓ
258. Ⓐ Ⓑ Ⓒ Ⓓ
259. Ⓐ Ⓑ Ⓒ Ⓓ

選択肢

(A) usually 副 たいてい

(B) once 接 いったん〜したら、〜するとすぐに 副 一度、かつて

(C) regularly 副 定期的に (D) steadily 副 着実に

正解・訳

256. (D)

過去3年間で、McMillan Frozen Dinnersは市場シェアを5パーセントから20パーセント近くにまで着実に伸ばしてきた。

257. (C)

上司は全代理人に対し、交通費報告書を定期的に更新して支払いの遅れを防ぐよう勧めている。

258. (A)

Penkalaさんはたいてい月曜日午前は空いているので、面会の予約をするのはそれが最も良い時だ。

259. (B)

ご登録が完了したら、Private Holdings Bankがあなたの個人識別番号をお送りします。

解説

257の空所に(A) usuallyを入れると「たいていは報告することを勧める」という意味になってしまうので、(C) regularly (定期的に) の方が妥当。**258**は、on Monday mornings「(毎週) 月曜日の午前は」とあるので、(A) usuallyが適切。

もう1問！

260. Over the past three years, McMillan Frozen Dinners has steadily ------- its market share from 5 percent to almost 20 percent.

(A) decreased (B) fostered (C) increased (D) escalated

▶▶▶ 解答は130ページ

Unit 5
Set 9

261. We regret to inform you that the sales representative ------- has already been filled.

262. The ------- is ideal for employees with young families as it has several good schools and large parks.

263. WX Motors' new electric car can be charged using a standard household power ------- .

264. During his tour to promote his latest book, Niles Dunbar made a brief ------- at the Annual Idaho Book Festival.

(A) position
(B) outlet
(C) location
(D) stop

261. Ⓐ Ⓑ Ⓒ Ⓓ
262. Ⓐ Ⓑ Ⓒ Ⓓ
263. Ⓐ Ⓑ Ⓒ Ⓓ
264. Ⓐ Ⓑ Ⓒ Ⓓ

選択肢

(A) position 名 職、ポジション　(B) outlet 名 直販店、（電気の）コンセント

(C) location 名 場所、立地、店舗

(D) stop 名 （旅行中の）滞在場所、滞在、立ち寄り、停車

解答・訳

261. (A)

残念ながら営業担当職には、すでに他の方が採用されてしまいました。

262. (C)

その立地は、良い学校や大きな公園があるため、子供がいる家庭を持つ従業員には理想的だ。

263. (B)

WX Motorsの新しい電気自動車は標準的な家庭用電源コンセントを使って充電できる。

264. (D)

Niles Dunbarは最新の自著を宣伝するためのツアー中に、年に1度のIdahoブックフェスティバルに短時間立ち寄りをした。

解説

263のoutletは元々「出口」という意味。「直営店」の他、電気の「差し込み口、コンセント」という意味でも使われる。**264**は空所の前のmakeを見た瞬間にmake a stop at ~（~に立ち寄る）という定型表現を想起して即答したいところだ。brief（短時間の）を足してmake a brief stop at ~にすると「~にちょっと立ち寄る」という意味になる。

もう1問！

265. We ------- to inform you that the sales representative position has already been filled.

(A) wish　(B) worry　(C) try　(C) regret

▶▶▶ 解答は130ページ

Unit 5

Set 10

266. Having served as a member of the sales department for five years, Ms. Danvers hopes to ------- to the customer service department.

267. This year's leadership workshop focused on effective ways to ------- work fairly among employees.

268. Most of the clerks ------- that the bank will be closed during the festival, but some may be required to come to work.

269. An advertising agency was hired to help ------- the government's new health program.

(A) delegate
(B) transfer
(C) assume
(D) promote

266. Ⓐ Ⓑ Ⓒ Ⓓ
267. Ⓐ Ⓑ Ⓒ Ⓓ
268. Ⓐ Ⓑ Ⓒ Ⓓ
269. Ⓐ Ⓑ Ⓒ Ⓓ

選択肢

(A) delegate 動 ～を委託する、委任する   (B) transfer 動 異動する

(C) assume 動 ～と想定する、見なす   (D) promote 動 ～を促進する

解答・訳

266. (B)

営業部員として5年間務めて、Danvers さんは顧客サービス部門に異動することを望んでいる。

267. (A)

今年のリーダーシップセミナーは、従業員間で仕事を公平に委託するための効果的な方法に焦点を絞った。

268. (C)

ほとんどの行員が、フェスティバルの期間中、銀行が休業することを想定しているが、一部の行員は出勤する必要があるだろう。

269. (D)

政府の新しい健康プログラムを促進するために広告代理店が雇われた。

解説

(B)のtransfer to ~はTOEIC頻出の表現。**266**では「～に異動する」という意味で使われているが、「～に移動する」「～に譲渡する」などの意味もある。(A)のdelegateは「自分の仕事や権限の一部を他の人に渡す」という意味。delegate a task to 人（<人>に仕事を任せる）のように使われる。

もう1問！

270. Most of the ------- assume that the bank will be closed during the festival, but some may be required to come to work.

(A) critics   (B) correspondents   (C) clerks   (D) shoppers

▶▶▶ 解答は130ページ

Unit 5
Set 11

271. Vera Donnelly was recently hired to manage the ------- renewal project of the East Bank area.

272. Due to security risks, customer files and password data must be kept in ------- locations.

273. Durant Towers is ------- to the Springfield Shopping Mall, which makes it a very convenient place to live.

274. As the Veresdale Research Facility is quite ------- , it is necessary for the company to supply worker accommodation.

(A) urban
(B) remote
(C) adjacent
(D) separate

271. (A) (B) (C) (D)
272. (A) (B) (C) (D)
273. (A) (B) (C) (D)
274. (A) (B) (C) (D)

選択肢

(A) urban 形 都会の、都市の　　(B) remote 形 人里離れた、可能性の低い

(C) adjacent 形 隣接した　　(D) separate 形 分かれた、別々の

正解・訳

271. (A)

Vera Donnelly は East Bank エリアの都市再開発プロジェクトを管理するために最近雇われた。

272. (D)

安全保障上、顧客ファイルとパスワードのデータは、別々の場所に保管されるべきである。

273. (C)

Durant Towers は Springfield Shopping Mall に隣接しているので、住むのにとても便利な場所となっている。

274. (B)

Veresdale の研究施設はかなり人里離れた場所にあるため、同社は労働者用宿泊施設を提供する必要がある。

解説

物・人の場所や位置関係を表す形容詞が並んでいる。**273.** 住むのに快適な場所は、ショッピングモールの「隣」なので (C) adjacent が正解。ちなみに TOEIC の最新のビルやマンションには、設備の整ったジムや美術館、水族館まで併設されることがある。

もう1問！

275. As the Veresdale Research Facility is quite remote, it is necessary for the company to supply worker ------- .

(A) storage　(B) invitation　(C) aid　(D) accommodation

▶▶▶ 解答は130ページ

225. (C)

Organizers have received ------- from Day's Catering and Dilbert Food Services, and they are likely to choose the former.

(A) bets　名 賭け
(B) statements　名 声明
(C) bids　名 入札
(D) billings　名 請求書

(→ p. 108、**221**)

230. (B)

Highway 86 has heavily congested ------- in the evenings and should be avoided when possible.

(A) route　名 ルート
(B) traffic　動 車の往来
(C) vehicle　名 乗り物
(D) pavement　動 舗装道路

(→ p. 110、**226**)

235. (B)

Film Now is an industry journal that ------- articles on the latest video equipment and profiles of outstanding new filmmakers.

(A) validates　動 ~を有効にする
(B) features　動 ~を目玉とする
(C) advocates　動 ~を指示する
(D) appears　動 現れる

(→ p. 112、**233**)

240. (C)

The council will probably adopt a ------- on the budget at the next town hall meeting this Friday.

(A) solution　名 解決
(B) method　名 方法
(C) resolution　名 決議案
(D) rule　名 規則

(→ p. 114、**239**)

245. (D)

Many stores sold out of the Dishlux frying pan in consequence of the ------- successful marketing campaign.

(A) generously　副 寛大にも
(B) barely　副 かろうじて
(C) inefficiently　副 非効率的に
(D) unexpectedly　副 予想外に

(→ p. 116、**243**)

250. (C)

Employees should discard their old security ------- as soon as they receive their new ones.

(A) gates 　名 ゲート、門
(B) vouchers 　名 金券
(C) badges 　名 バッジ、許可証
(D) features 　名 特徴

(→ p. 118、**249**)

255. (A)

It is not feasible to expand the company until we ------- the labor shortage issue.

(A) resolve 　動 ～を解決する
(B) postpone 　動 ～を後回しにする
(C) intrigue 　動 ～の興味をそそる
(D) concentrate 　動 ～を集中させる

(→ p. 120、**251**)

260. (C)

Over the past three years, McMillan Frozen Dinners has steadily ------- its market share from 5 percent to almost 20 percent.

(A) decreased 　動 減らした
(B) fostered 　動 育てた
(C) increased 　動 増やした
(D) escalated 　動 段階的に上昇した

(→ p. 122、**256**)

265. (D)

We ------- to inform you that the sales representative position has already been filled.

(A) wish 　動 ～を希望する
(B) worry 　動 ～を心配する
(C) try 　動 ～を試す
(D) regret 　動 ～を残念に思う

(→ p. 124、**261**)

270. (C)

Most of the ------- assume that the bank will be closed during the festival, but some may be required to come to work.

(A) critics 　名 批評家たち
(B) correspondents 　名 特派員たち
(C) clerks 　名 事務員たち
(D) shoppers 　名 買い物客たち

(→ p. 126、**268**)

275. (D)

As the Veresdale Research Facility is quite remote, it is necessary for the company to supply worker ------- .

(A) storage 　名 収納
(B) invitation 　名 招待
(C) aid 　名 援助
(D) accommodation 　名 宿泊施設

(→ p. 128、**274**)

Unit 6

Set 1

276. ------- there are no more construction delays, the new hospital will not be completed by the deadline.

277. ------- working as a marketing assistant, Ms. Han has asked to join the accounting department.

278. ------- you have not heard, the monthly meeting has been postponed until August 30.

279. ------- the order is submitted by noon, Hamilton Restaurant Supplies should be able to complete delivery by 5:00 P.M.

(A) Rather than
(B) As long as
(C) In case
(D) Even if

276. Ⓐ Ⓑ Ⓒ Ⓓ
277. Ⓐ Ⓑ Ⓒ Ⓓ
278. Ⓐ Ⓑ Ⓒ Ⓓ
279. Ⓐ Ⓑ Ⓒ Ⓓ

選択肢

(A) Rather than ～よりむしろ　(B) As long as ～する限り

(C) In case ～するといけないので、～の場合の用心に

(D) Even if たとえ～でも

正解・訳

276. (D)

<u>たとえ</u>これ以上の建設の遅れがなく<u>ても</u>、新しい病院は期限までに完成しない。

277. (A)

Han さんはマーケティングアシスタントとして働く<u>より、むしろ</u>経理部に入りたいと依願した。

278. (C)

お耳に入っていない<u>といけないので</u>（申し上げますが）、月例会議は8月30日まで延期になりました。

279. (B)

正午までに発注されている<u>限り</u>、Hamilton Restaurant Supplies は午後5時までに配送を完了できるはずだ。

解説

接続表現の問題なので、カンマ前後の内容と関係を押さえよう。カンマ前後には節があるが、**277**のカンマの前のみ名詞（句）だ。このような使い方ができるのは、(A) Rather thanのみ。(C)のIn caseを名詞と使う場合は、in case of ~ とする必要がある。

もう１問！

280. As long as the order is ------ by noon, Hamilton Restaurant Supplies should be able to complete delivery by 5:00 P.M.

(A) canceled　(B) expressed　(C) submitted　(D) commenced

▶▶▶ 解答は153ページ

Unit 6

Set 2

281. The end of the fiscal year is always an extremely busy time for an ------- .

282. After a discussion with his ------- , Mr. Reed was confident that his product does not infringe on any valid patents.

283. The ------- hired to design the new theater suggested adding an underground parking garage.

284. The new eatery is now ready for a visit by the health ------- before its grand opening next week.

問題281~285 Unit 6

(A) architect
(B) accountant
(C) inspector
(D) attorney

281. Ⓐ Ⓑ Ⓒ Ⓓ
282. Ⓐ Ⓑ Ⓒ Ⓓ
283. Ⓐ Ⓑ Ⓒ Ⓓ
284. Ⓐ Ⓑ Ⓒ Ⓓ

名詞14

選択肢

(A) architect 名 建築家　　(B) accountant 名 会計士

(C) inspector 名 検査官　　(D) attorney 名 弁護士

解答・訳

281. (B)

会計年度末は会計士にとって、常にとても忙しい時期である。

282. (D)

Reedさんは弁護士と話した後、自分の商品が有効な特許を侵害していないということに自信を持った。

283. (A)

新しい劇場を設計するために雇われた建築家は、地下駐車場を追加することを提案した。

284. (C)

その新しい飲食店は、来週のグランドオープンを前に、衛生検査官による訪問への準備ができている。

eatery: 飲食店

解説

選択肢には職業に関連するTOEIC頻出の名詞が並んでいる。文全体をしっかり読み、文脈やキーワードから正答を特定しよう。**281** は the fiscal year（会計年度）を見た時点で、関連する accountant（会計士）にたどり着きたいところ。**283** は design the new theater（新しい劇場を設計する）から architect（建築家）を選択できる。

もう1問！

285. The architect ------- to design the new theater suggested adding an underground parking garage.

(A) planned (B) hired (C) designed (D) gained

▶▶▶ 解答は153ページ

Unit 6

Set 3

286. If you are using the car rental service for the first time, an additional registration fee may ------- .

287. Covert Coal's policy requires staff members to ------- the company two months before they intend to resign from their positions.

288. An inspector will visit the photography studio to ensure that chemical disposal practices ------- with state regulations.

問題 286～290 Unit 6

289. An e-mail is sent to clients when they sign up in order to ------- that they have given the correct contact information.

(A) comply
(B) verify
(C) apply
(D) notify

286. Ⓐ Ⓑ Ⓒ Ⓓ
287. Ⓐ Ⓑ Ⓒ Ⓓ
288. Ⓐ Ⓑ Ⓒ Ⓓ
289. Ⓐ Ⓑ Ⓒ Ⓓ

選択肢

(A) comply 　動 順守する、従う 　　(B) verify 　動 ～を確認する、実証する

(C) apply 　動 適用される 　　　　(D) notify 　動 ～に通知する、告知する

解答・訳

286. (C)

レンタカーサービスを初めて使用する場合は、追加の登録料が適用される場合がある。

287. (D)

Covert Coalの方針では、従業員は辞職予定の2カ月前に会社に通知する必要がある。

288. (A)

検査官は、化学物質の処分方法が州の規制に従っていることを確認するために、写真スタジオを訪れるだろう。

disposal: 処分、廃棄

289. (B)

正しい連絡先情報を提供したことを確認するために、サインアップ時に電子メールがクライアントに送信される。

解説

287の(D) notifyは「～に正式に伝える、知らせる」という意味の堅い表現。重要なことを正式に通知するといった場面で使われる。**289**の(A) comply with ～は「～に従う、適合する」というTOEIC頻出の表現だ。**289**の(B) verifyは「～が正しいか（正確か）どうかを検証する」＝「確認する」という意味。

もう1問！

290. Covert Coal's policy requires staff members to notify the company two months before they intend to ------- from their positions.

(A) quit　(B) assign　(C) disappoint　(D) resign

▶▶▶ 解答は153ページ

Unit 6

Set 4

291. The ------- manner in which Ms. Tao rearranged the lighting in the studio showed that she was an experienced photographer.

292. Please insure any ------- items as Michaelson Shipping accepts no responsibility for packages damaged in transit.

293. The carpet for the main entrance area should be ------- enough to withstand heavy traffic.

294. Product manager Sayuri Ando was praised for her contribution to the company's ------- growth last quarter.

(A) durable
(B) sophisticated
(C) fragile
(D) solid

291. Ⓐ Ⓑ Ⓒ Ⓓ
292. Ⓐ Ⓑ Ⓒ Ⓓ
293. Ⓐ Ⓑ Ⓒ Ⓓ
294. Ⓐ Ⓑ Ⓒ Ⓓ

形容詞13

選択肢

(A) durable 形 耐久性のある　　(B) sophisticated 形 洗練された、高機能の

(C) fragile 形 壊れやすい　　(D) solid 形 確かな、堅調な

解答・訳

291. (B)

Taoさんがスタジオの照明の位置を変えた際の洗練された物腰は、彼女が経験豊かな写真家であることを表していた。

292. (C)

Michaelson Shippingは輸送中に破損した荷物について一切責任を負わないため、壊れやすい品物には保険をかけてください。

insure: ～に保険を掛ける

293. (A)

中央玄関部分のカーペットは、人の往来の多さに耐えられるよう、十分に耐久性のあるものでなくてはならない。

294. (D)

プロダクトマネージャーのSayuri Andoは、前四半期に会社の堅調な成長に貢献したことを称賛された。

解説

(B) sophisticatedは291のように人を形容する語として「洗練された」という意味でよく使われるが、機械や技術などに関して「高機能の、高性能の」という意味でも使われる。292のfragile item（壊れやすい品物）もTOEIC頻出の語だ。

もう1問！

295. Please insure any fragile items as Michaelson Shipping accepts no responsibility for packages ------- in transit.

(A) occurred　(B) retrieved　(C) damaged　(D) sent

▶▶▶ 解答は153ページ

Unit 6

Set 5

296. Mr. Carson cannot meet the film producer today because he is ------- busy working on his manuscript.

297. Due to his tight schedule, Mr. Thompson ------- has time to attend section meetings.

298. Sales increased by ------- over 2 percent following the expensive advertising campaign.

299. After the major sporting event, demand for high-resolution televisions increased -------, and the factory was unable to keep up.

(A) rarely
(B) suddenly
(C) just
(D) very

296. Ⓐ Ⓑ Ⓒ Ⓓ
297. Ⓐ Ⓑ Ⓒ Ⓓ
298. Ⓐ Ⓑ Ⓒ Ⓓ
299. Ⓐ Ⓑ Ⓒ Ⓓ

選択肢

(A) rarely 副 めったに～ない   (B) suddenly 副 突然に
(C) just 副 たった～だけ、ちょっと   (D) very 副 とても

解答・訳

296. (D)

Carson さんは、原稿の執筆でとても忙しいため、映画プロデューサーと今日会うことができない。
manuscript: 原稿

297. (A)

過密なスケジュールのため、Thompson さんは部門会議に出席する時間がめったにない。

298. (C)

費用のかかる広告キャンペーンの後、売上は2パーセントをわずかに超える程度、増加した。

299. (B)

大きなスポーツ大会の後、高解像度テレビの需要が突然増加し、工場は（その需要に）対応することができなかった。

解説

(A) rarely は頻度を表す副詞。起こる確率のかなり低いことを表し、本動詞の前に置かれる。同義語に seldom があるが、こちらはよりフォーマルな場面で使われる。(B) suddenly（急に）には、時間的に急に（quickly）というだけでなく、予期せぬタイミングで不意に（unexpectedly）という意味合いもある。

もう1問！

300. After the major sporting event, demand for high-resolution televisions increased suddenly, and the factory was unable to ------- up.

(A) step   (B) take   (C) make   (D) keep

▶▶▶ 解答は153ページ

Unit 6

Set 6

301. The ------- to the library's east wing will take at least four months to complete.

302. The employees will receive the results of their annual performance ------- by e-mail.

303. To access the main building, please present your ------- badge at the entrance.

304. The ------- process for the conference is simple and can be completed on the Web site.

問題301〜305 Unit **6**

(A) extension
(B) evaluation
(C) identification
(D) registration

301. (A) (B) (C) (D)
302. (A) (B) (C) (D)
303. (A) (B) (C) (D)
304. (A) (B) (C) (D)

名詞15

選択肢

(A) extension 名 拡張、増築

(B) evaluation 名 評価

(C) identification 名 身分証明 (証)

(D) registration 名 登録

解答・訳

301. (A)

図書館の東館の拡張は、完了までに少なくとも4カ月かかるだろう。

302. (B)

従業員は年次業績評価の結果をメールで受け取るだろう。

303. (C)

本館に立ち入るには、入り口でご自身の身分証明証を提示してください。

304. (D)

会議への登録手続きは簡単で、ウェブサイト上で完了できる。

解説

301の(A) extension to ～ (～の拡張) は建物の増築だけでなく、「期間の延長」を表す際にも使われる。**302**の(B) performance evaluation (業績評価) はTOEIC頻出の表現で、performance evaluation form (業績評価表) という語句もよく登場する。

もう1問！

305. To access the main building, please ------- your identification badge at the entrance.

    (A) place (B) apply (C) present (D) see

▶▶▶ 解答は154ページ

Unit 6

Set 7

306. The Dalton 100 alarm clock is small and light, which makes it ------- for taking on business trips.

307. Because they have few chances to sit down, Grand Willow Medical Clinic advises nurses to wear ------- shoes.

308. The Philomena Street office is only ------- by car as there are no train stations or bus stops nearby.

309. Silvio's serves simple but ------- Italian meals to its loyal customers seven days a week.

問題306-310 Unit 6

(A) accessible
(B) comfortable
(C) handy
(D) authentic

306. Ⓐ Ⓑ Ⓒ Ⓓ
307. Ⓐ Ⓑ Ⓒ Ⓓ
308. Ⓐ Ⓑ Ⓒ Ⓓ
309. Ⓐ Ⓑ Ⓒ Ⓓ

形容詞14

選択肢

(A) accessible 形 （場所が）到達できる　　(B) comfortable 形 快適な

(C) handy 形 便利な、役に立つ　　(D) authentic 形 本物の、真正の

解答・訳

306. (C)

Dalton 100の目覚まし時計は小さくて軽いので、出張に持っていくのに<u>便利だ</u>。

307. (B)

座る機会がほとんどないため、Grand Willow Medical Clinicは看護師に<u>快適な</u>靴を履くよう勧めている。

308. (A)

Philomena 通りの事務所は、近くに駅やバス停がないため、車でのみ<u>アクセスできる</u>。

309. (D)

Silvio'sは、週に7日、シンプルでありながら<u>本格的な</u>イタリア料理を得意客に提供している。

解説

306の(B) handy for ~ は「～に便利な、役立つ」という意味の定型表現。handy は「手軽に使える便利さ」を表すのに対し、同義語のuseful は「道具として役に立つ便利さ」を表す。(D)のauthentic は「複製されたものではない、本物の」という意味。**309**では「（料理が）本格的な、本場の」という意味で使われている。

もう1問！

310. The Philomena Street office is only accessible by car as there are no train stations or bus stops ------- .

(A) closely　(B) nearby　(C) conveniently　(D) neighborly

▶▶▶ 解答は154ページ

Unit 6

Set 8

311. A new bridge is being built to ------- traffic congestion in the city center.

312. Ms. Michaels was asked to ------- a group of new hires during their first week at the company.

313. The mechanic is unable to accurately ------- the repair cost because some parts have already been discontinued.

314. To ------- your new credit card, please call our customer support line at 555-9934.

(A) alleviate
(B) supervise
(C) estimate
(D) activate

311. Ⓐ Ⓑ Ⓒ Ⓓ
312. Ⓐ Ⓑ Ⓒ Ⓓ
313. Ⓐ Ⓑ Ⓒ Ⓓ
314. Ⓐ Ⓑ Ⓒ Ⓓ

選択肢

(A) alleviate 動 ～を緩和する、軽減する　(B) supervise 動 ～を監督する
(C) estimate 動 ～を見積もる　(D) activate 動 ～を作動させる、有効にする

解答・訳

311. (A)
市内中心部の交通渋滞を緩和するために、新しい橋が建設されている。

312. (B)
Michaelsさんは新入社員のグループを、初出社の週の間、監督するように頼まれた。

313. (C)
一部の部品の製造が打ち切られたため、整備士は修理費用を正確に見積もることができない。

314. (D)
新しいクレジットカードを有効にするには、カスタマーサポート555-9934番にお電話ください。

解説

(A)のalleviateは「～を緩和する」。**311**のtraffic congestion（交通渋滞）はTOEIC頻出の表現。(B) superviseは元々「上から見る」という意味で、そこから**312**のように「～を監督する」という意味で使われている。人の監督だけでなく、supervise construction（建設を管理する）のようにも使われる。

もう1問！

315. The mechanic is unable to accurately estimate the repair cost because some parts have already been ------- .

　　(A) discontinued　(B) terminated　(C) cleared　(D) finished

▶▶▶ 解答は154ページ

Unit 6

Set 9

316. Considering their excellent reputation for reliability, the TFG televisions are ------- inexpensive to buy.

317. Because our tire diagnostic tools usually spend many months on store shelves, batteries are sold -------.

318. Due to his fame in the art world, Max Day's exhibitions ------- draw large crowds.

319. As expected, there are ------- six locations that might be considered for the new corporate headquarters.

問題316～320 Unit **6**

(A) surprisingly
(B) typically
(C) separately
(D) potentially

316. Ⓐ Ⓑ Ⓒ Ⓓ
317. Ⓐ Ⓑ Ⓒ Ⓓ
318. Ⓐ Ⓑ Ⓒ Ⓓ
319. Ⓐ Ⓑ Ⓒ Ⓓ

選択肢

(A) surprisingly 副 驚くほどに　　(B) typically 副 通常は、典型的に

(C) separately 副 別に　　(D) potentially 副 潜在的に

解答・訳

316. (A)

信頼性に関する優れた評判を考慮すると、TFGのテレビは驚くほど安価に購入できる。

317. (C)

通常、わが社のタイヤ診断ツールは何カ月も店頭に置かれるため、バッテリーは別にして売られている。

318. (B)

アート界での名声により、Max Dayの展示会は通常は大勢の観客を引き付ける。

319. (D)

予想されているように、新しい本社として検討されうる場所が潜在的に6カ所ある。

解説

(A) surprisingly は「(通常ではない状態が思いがけなく起きて) 驚くほどに」という意味。316のように surprisingly inexpensive (驚くほど安価な) や surprisingly accurate (驚くほど正確な) など形容詞の前によく置かれる。(D) potentially は「これから発展して実現する力を秘めている」＝「潜在的な」という意味。

もう1問！

320. Due to his fame in the art world, Max Day's exhibitions typically ------- large crowds.

(A) occupy　(B) accept　(C) capture　(D) draw

▶▶▶ 解答は154ページ

Unit 6

Set 10

321. Staff training requires a considerable ------- of time and money from the employer.

322. Employees will receive full ------- for any expenses associated with business trips or entertaining clients.

323. Thanks to the new CEO's innovative marketing strategy, sales showed a significant ------- over the previous year.

324. Todd McAvey worked in product ------- , where he helped design many of the company's most popular devices.

(A) reimbursement
(B) development
(C) improvement
(D) investment

321. Ⓐ Ⓑ Ⓒ Ⓓ
322. Ⓐ Ⓑ Ⓒ Ⓓ
323. Ⓐ Ⓑ Ⓒ Ⓓ
324. Ⓐ Ⓑ Ⓒ Ⓓ

名詞16

選択肢
....

(A) reimbursement [名] (費用などの) 返金　(B) development [名] 開発

(C) improvement [名] 改善　(D) investment [名] 投資

解答・訳
....

321. (D)

スタッフのトレーニングには、雇用主による多大な時間と費用の投資が必要だ。
considerable: かなりの

322. (A)

従業員は、出張や顧客の接待に関連する費用については全額返金を受け取るだろう。

323. (C)

新しいCEOの革新的なマーケティング戦略のおかげで、売上高は前年に比べて大幅に改善した。

324. (B)

Todd McAveyは製品開発部門に勤務し、その会社の最も人気のある多くの装置の設計を手掛けた。

解説
....

(A)のreimbursementはTOEICに特に頻出する語。**322**のように、「(立て替えて支払ったお金の) 返金、払い戻し」という意味でよく使われる。**324**は空所の前のproductを見た瞬間に、頻出のproduct development (商品開発) という定型表現を想起して解答できるようにしたい。

もう1問！
....

325. Employees will receive full refund for any expenses ------- with business trips or entertaining clients.

(A) related　(B) associated　(C) prepaid　(D) accompanied

▶▶▶ 解答は154ページ

Unit 6
Set 11

326. If in doubt about how to proceed, employees should ------- the guidelines listed in the employee manual.

327. Dan Thompson was asked to ------- out invitations to the annual client appreciation dinner by registered mail.

328. Ferry passengers must ------- through a security checkpoint before they travel from Xiamen to Gulangyu Island.

329. Calister Hotels ------- to business travelers by providing a desk in each room.

(A) cater
(B) observe
(C) send
(D) pass

問題 326〜330 Unit 6

326. Ⓐ Ⓑ Ⓒ Ⓓ
327. Ⓐ Ⓑ Ⓒ Ⓓ
328. Ⓐ Ⓑ Ⓒ Ⓓ
329. Ⓐ Ⓑ Ⓒ Ⓓ

選択肢

(A) cater 動 ～（要求など）に応じる

(B) observe 動 ～（法律や規則）を守る、遵守する、よく見る、観察する

(C) send 動 送る (D) pass 動 通過する

解答・訳

326. (B)

進め方に疑問がある場合、従業員は従業員マニュアルに記載されているガイドラインを遵守する必要がある。

327. (C)

Dan Thompsonは、年次顧客感謝ディナーへの招待状を書留郵便で送るように求められた。

328. (D)

フェリーの乗客は、XiamenからGulangyu Islandに移動する前に、検問所を通過する必要がある。

329. (A)

Calister Hotelsは、各部屋に机を設置することでビジネス旅行者に対応している。

解説

send out ～は「～（手紙など）を発送する」という意味の頻出表現。**327**のsend out invitations（招待状）のように多くの人に何かを送る際に使われる。(A)のcaterは「（料理を）仕出しする」という意味でよく使われるが、**329**のcater to ～（～[要求など]に応じる）の用法も覚えておこう。

もう1問！

330. Dan Thompson was asked to send out invitations to the annual client ------- dinner by registered mail.

   (A) enterprise (B) appreciation (C) accountability (D) innovation

▶▶▶ 解答は154ページ

Unit 6 　もう1問！ 解答一覧

※問題文の訳は(→　)内のページ・番号を参照してください

280. (C)

As long as the order is ------- by noon, Hamilton Restaurant Supplies should be able to complete delivery by 5:00 P.M.

(A) canceled 　動 ～をキャンセルした　　(B) expressed 　動 ～を表現した
(C) submitted 　動 ～を提出した　　(D) commenced 　動 ～を開始した

(→ p. 132、**279**)

285. (B)

The architect ------- to design the new theater suggested adding an underground parking garage.

(A) planned 　動 計画された　　(B) hired 　動 雇われた
(C) designed 　動 設計された　　(D) gained 　動 得られた

(→ p. 134、**283**)

290. (D)

Covert Coal's policy requires staff members to notify the company two months before they intend to ------- from their positions.

(A) quit 　動 ～を辞める　　(B) assign 　動 ～を割り当てる
(C) disappoint 　動 ～を失望させる　　(D) resign 　動 辞職する、～を辞める

(→ p. 136、**287**)

295. (C)

Please insure any fragile items as Michaelson Shipping accepts no responsibility for packages ------- in transit.

(A) occurred 　動 発生した　　(B) retrieved 　動 回収された
(C) damaged 　動 損傷を受けた　　(D) sent 　動 送られた

(→ p. 138、**292**)

300. (D)

After the major sporting event, demand for high-resolution televisions increased suddenly, and the factory was unable to ------- up.

(A) step 　動 踏む、前に出る　　(B) take 　動 取る、～を要する
(C) make 　動 作る、なる　　(D) keep 　動 保つ、続ける

(→ p. 140、**299**)

305. (C)

To access the main building, please ------- your identification badge at the entrance.

(A) place 　動 ～を置く (B) apply 　動 ～を適用する
(C) present 　動 ～を提示する (D) see 　動 ～を見る

310. (B)

The Philomena Street office is only accessible by car as there are no train stations or bus stops -------.

(A) closely 　副 密接に (B) nearby 　副 近くに
(C) conveniently 　副 便利に (D) neighborly 　形 隣人らしい

(→ p. 144、**308**)

315. (A)

The mechanic is unable to accurately estimate the repair cost because some parts have already been ------- .

(A) discontinued 　動 製造中止された (B) terminated 　動 終わった
(C) cleared 　動 取り除いた (D) finished 　動 終わった

(→ p. 146、**313**)

320. (D)

Due to his fame in the art world, Max Day's exhibitions typically ------- large crowds.

(A) occupy 　動 ～を占める (B) accept 　動 ～を受け入れる
(C) capture 　動 ～をとらえる (D) draw 　動 ～を引き付ける

(→ p. 148、**318**)

325. (B)

Employees will receive full refund for any expenses ------- with business trips or entertaining clients.

(A) related 　動 関連した (B) associated 　動 関連した
(C) prepaid 　動 すでに支払われた (D) accompanied 　動 伴われた

(→ p. 150、**322**)

330. (B)

Dan Thompson was asked to send out invitations to the annual client ------- dinner by registered mail.

(A) enterprise 　名 企業 (B) appreciation 　名 感謝
(C) accountability 　名 説明責任 (D) innovation 　名 革新

(→ p. 152、**327**)

Unit 7

Set 1

331. Mr. Barkworth arrived at the event just ------- time to give his speech.

332. The credit card company recommends that customers check their receipts ------- their monthly statements online.

333. Important information regarding printer maintenance is included ------- Page 12 of the user manual.

334. Attendees at the banquet were asked to choose ------- a number of food and beverage options.

(A) on
(B) among
(C) against
(D) in

331. Ⓐ Ⓑ Ⓒ Ⓓ
332. Ⓐ Ⓑ Ⓒ Ⓓ
333. Ⓐ Ⓑ Ⓒ Ⓓ
334. Ⓐ Ⓑ Ⓒ Ⓓ

前置詞04

選択肢

(A) on 前 ～に、～の上に   (B) among 前 ～の間で、～の中で

(C) against 前 ～と対照して   (D) in 前 ～の時に、～の中で

解答・訳

331. (C)
Barkworthさんは、スピーチをするのにぎりぎり間に合ってイベントに到着した。

332. (C)
そのクレジットカード会社は、領収書を毎月のオンライン明細書と照らし合わせて確認するよう顧客に推奨している。

333. (A)
プリンターのメンテナンスに関する重要な情報は、ユーザーマニュアルの12ページに記載されている。

334. (B)
宴会の出席者は、多くの食べ物と飲み物の選択肢の中から選ぶように求められた。

解説

空所前後の語句との相性を確認。**331**はjust in time（ぎりぎりで間に合って）という定番表現だ。(C) againstは「～に反対して」という意味でよく使われるが、**332**のように2つのものを対比するときにも使われる。(B) amongは「（複数のもの）の中で」という意味なので、後ろには**334**のように複数形の名詞が来る。

もう1問！

335. The credit card company recommends that customers check their receipts against their monthly ------- online.

(A) status (B) purchases (C) statements (D) calculations

▶▶▶ 解答は177ページ

Unit 7
Set 2

336. Accountants at Freeman Associates read all the major industry journals to ensure that their ------- advice is current.

337. With the fall in sales, most of our employees will be looking at ------- vacation this year.

338. Given her unique background in ------- photography, we believe Ms. Larson will make an excellent graphic designer.

339. Some engineers that worked at Omega Ware Devices left for more ------- jobs at larger companies.

問題336~340 Unit **7**

(A) commercial
(B) lucrative
(C) budget
(D) financial

336. Ⓐ Ⓑ Ⓒ Ⓓ
337. Ⓐ Ⓑ Ⓒ Ⓓ
338. Ⓐ Ⓑ Ⓒ Ⓓ
339. Ⓐ Ⓑ Ⓒ Ⓓ

形容詞15

選択肢

(A) commercial 形 商用の、商業の

(B) lucrative 形 実入りのいい、利益の上がる

(C) budget 名 予算 形 お買い得の、格安の (D) financial 形 財務の

解答・訳

336. (D)

Freeman Associatesの会計士は、彼らの<u>財務</u>アドバイスが最新であることを確実にするために、主要な業界誌をすべて読んでいる。

337. (C)

売上減少により、わが社の従業員の多くは今年<u>格安</u>の休暇を検討することになるだろう。

338. (A)

彼女の<u>商業</u>写真界でのユニークな経歴を考えると、Larsonさんは優れたグラフィックデザイナーになると思う。

339. (B)

Omega Ware Devicesで働いていた一部のエンジニアは退職し、より大きな企業でもっと<u>実入りのいい</u>仕事に就いた。

解説

(A)のcommercialは、名詞ではおなじみの「(テレビ・ラジオなどの) コマーシャル」という意味だが、**338**のように形容詞では「物の売買に関連して利益を生もうとする」=「商用の、商業の」という意味で使われる。(B)のlucrativeは「もうかる、多額の利益を生み出す」という意味。同義語はprofitable (もうかる、利益になる)。

もう1問！

340. Accountants at Freeman Associates read all the major industry ------- to ensure that their financial advice is current.

(A) timelines (B) journals (C) standards (D) merchandise

▶▶▶ 解答は177ページ

Unit 7
Set 3

341. Mr. Allan posted another advertisement after ------- few applicants responded to his original job ad.

342. According to her résumé, Ms. Cahill ------- worked as an interior decorator.

343. The changes to the design will ------- make the new appliances easier to clean and more dependable.

344. VGT brand auto parts are not ------- sold at retail stores and should be ordered online.

(A) previously
(B) commonly
(C) hopefully
(D) relatively

Unit
7
問題341~345

341. Ⓐ Ⓑ Ⓒ Ⓓ
342. Ⓐ Ⓑ Ⓒ Ⓓ
343. Ⓐ Ⓑ Ⓒ Ⓓ
344. Ⓐ Ⓑ Ⓒ Ⓓ

選択肢

(A) previously 副 以前に

(B) commonly 副 一般に、通常

(C) hopefully 副 願わくは、うまくいけば

(D) relatively 副 比較的

解答・訳

341. (D)

比較的少数の応募者が最初の求人広告に応答した後で、Allanさんは別の広告を掲載した。

342. (A)

履歴書によれば、Cahillさんは以前インテリアデザイナーとして働いていた。

343. (C)

設計の変更により、新しい電化製品のクリーニングが容易になり、うまくいけば信頼性を高めることになる。

appliance: 電化製品

344. (B)

VGTブランドの自動車部品は通常は小売店では販売されておらず、オンラインで注文する必要がある。

解説

(D) relatively は「他の類似のものと比べて、違いの程度がそれなりに大きい」ことを表現する際に使われる。**341**のrelatively few（比較的少数の）やrelatively easy（比較的簡単な）のように後ろに形容詞を置いて使われる。**342**の(A) previously worked（以前働いていた）も頻出表現だ。

もう1問！

345. The changes to the design will hopefully make the new -------
easier to clean and more dependable.

(A) appliances (B) operations (C) signatures (D) manuscripts

▶▶▶ 解答は177ページ

Unit 7

Set 4

346. As the projector was still covered by a ------- , we were able to demand a replacement when it broke down.

347. Please view our 10-minute online ------- to learn how to properly use the camera's various functions.

348. If a ------- is received from a customer, it should be forwarded to the public relations department immediately.

349. The revised shipping ------- has drastically reduced the number of delivery errors.

問題346-350 Unit 7

(A) tutorial
(B) procedure
(C) complaint
(D) warranty

346. Ⓐ Ⓑ Ⓒ Ⓓ
347. Ⓐ Ⓑ Ⓒ Ⓓ
348. Ⓐ Ⓑ Ⓒ Ⓓ
349. Ⓐ Ⓑ Ⓒ Ⓓ

名詞17

選択肢

(A) tutorial 名 チュートリアル (B) procedure 名 手順

(C) complaint 名 苦情、クレーム (D) warranty 名 保証

解答・訳

346. (D)

プロジェクターはまだ保証期間中であったため、故障した時に交換を要求することができた。

347. (A)

カメラのさまざまな機能を適切に使用する方法を学ぶには、10分間のオンラインチュートリアルをご覧ください。

348. (C)

顧客から苦情を受け取った場合、すぐに広報部門に転送する必要がある。

349. (B)

改訂された配送手順により、誤配の件数が大幅に減少した。

解説

346は covered by a warranty で「保証によってカバーされている」＝「保証期間中の」という意味になる。他に under warranty（保証期間中の）も使われる。(A) tutorial は「個別指導、指導書」という意味だが日本語でも「チュートリアル」とそのまま使われることが多い。**347**の online tutorial は、インターネット上で見られる手引書のこと。

もう1問！

350. As the projector was still covered by a warranty, we were able to demand a ------- when it broke down.

(A) reward (B) solution (C) replacement (D) deposit

▶▶▶ 解答は177ページ

Unit 7

Set 5

351. Please find a self-addressed return envelope -------
for you to use when you return the signed contract
to Amelia Publishing.

352. The office rental agreement was ------- when the
tenant asked for additional parking spaces.

353. If the storage space is not securely covered,
construction materials may be ------- to bad
weather.

354. Advertising space in *The Dalton Bugle* is expensive
as it is one of the country's most widely -------
newspapers.

(A) enclosed
(B) distributed
(C) modified
(D) exposed

351. Ⓐ Ⓑ Ⓒ Ⓓ
352. Ⓐ Ⓑ Ⓒ Ⓓ
353. Ⓐ Ⓑ Ⓒ Ⓓ
354. Ⓐ Ⓑ Ⓒ Ⓓ

選択肢

(A) enclosed 動 同封された   (B) distributed 動 配付された

(C) modified 動 修正された   (D) exposed 動 さらされた

解答・訳

351. (A)

署名済みの契約書をAmelia Publishingに返送される際にご利用いただける、同封された宛先記入済みの返信用封筒をご確認ください。

self-addressed: 宛先記入済みの

352. (C)

テナントが追加の駐車スペースを要望したときに、オフィス賃貸契約が修正された。

353. (D)

保管スペースがしっかりと覆われていない場合、建設資材が悪天候にさらされる可能性がある。

354. (B)

*The Dalton Bugle*は国内で最も広く配られている新聞の1つであるため、その広告スペースは高価だ。

解説

選択肢には動詞の過去分詞が並んでいる。(A)を入れた**351**のplease find ... enclosedは、同封したものを確認するよう相手に促す際に使う鉄板の表現。**352**に入る(C)の原形 modifyは、「より良い状態にするために一部分を修正する」という意味合いで使われる。(D)を入れた**353**のbe exposed to ~ (~にさらされる)もTOEIC頻出の定型表現だ。

もう1問！

355. If the storage space is not ------- covered, construction materials may be exposed to bad weather.

    (A) closely (B) evenly (C) exactly (D) securely

▶▶▶ 解答は177ページ

Unit 7

Set 6

356. Before purchase, please check the specifications of your computer to make sure that this device is entirely ------- .

357. Tullamore Dishware is carefully packaged to ensure that every item arrives at its destination completely ------- .

358. Visitors to the factory are asked to wear ------- gloves, which they can put in the trash at the end of the tour.

359. At Aprico Appliances, customers can return their order within 12 months of purchase if an item is ------- .

問題356~360 Unit 7

(A) disposable
(B) defective
(C) intact
(D) compatible

356. Ⓐ Ⓑ Ⓒ Ⓓ
357. Ⓐ Ⓑ Ⓒ Ⓓ
358. Ⓐ Ⓑ Ⓒ Ⓓ
359. Ⓐ Ⓑ Ⓒ Ⓓ

形容詞16

選択肢

(A) disposable 形 使い捨てできる　　(B) defective 形 欠陥がある
(C) intact 形 損傷を受けていない　　(D) compatible 形 互換性のある

解答・訳

356. (D)

購入する前にお持ちのコンピューターの仕様を確認して、この機器が完全に<u>互換性があ</u>ることを確認してください。
specification: 仕様（書）

357. (C)

Tullamoreの食器類は、全ての品物が完全に<u>無傷</u>の状態で目的地に到着するように、慎重に梱包されている。

358. (A)

工場への訪問者は<u>使い捨て</u>の手袋を着用するよう求められ、それはツアーの最後にゴミ箱に捨てることができる。

359. (B)

Aprico Appliancesでは、商品に<u>欠陥がある</u>場合、購入後12カ月以内ならば顧客はその注文品を返品できる。

解説

(C) intactは物についても、人の評判などについても使える。(D) compatibleは、**356**のように機械について使うと「互換性がある」という意味になるが、人との関係に関しては「相性が良い」という意味で使われる。(B) defectiveはdefective item（欠陥商品）という定型表現も覚えておきたい。

もう1問！

360. Before purchase, please check the specifications of your computer to make sure that this device is ------- compatible.

　　　(A) entirely　(B) hardly　(C) environmentally　(D) genuinely

▶▶▶ 解答は178ページ

Unit 7

Set 7

361. Some people can work well with background music, ------- others need quiet surroundings to concentrate.

362. We should review the building plans this afternoon, ------- the contractor will be here at the factory at 8:00 A.M. tomorrow.

363. The restaurant looked strikingly classical, ------- it was built only six months ago.

364. The Regent Hotel has been designed ------- two-thirds of its rooms have an ocean view.

(A) as
(B) so that
(C) although
(D) while

361. Ⓐ Ⓑ Ⓒ Ⓓ
362. Ⓐ Ⓑ Ⓒ Ⓓ
363. Ⓐ Ⓑ Ⓒ Ⓓ
364. Ⓐ Ⓑ Ⓒ Ⓓ

選択肢

(A) as 接 ～なので

(B) so that ～になるように

(C) although 接 ～にも関わらず、だけれども

(D) while 接 しかし一方で

解答・訳

361. (D)

BGMが流れていてもうまく仕事ができる人もいる一方で、集中するために静かな環境が必要な人もいる。

362. (A)

明日午前8時に請負業者が工場に到着するので、今日の午後に建築計画を精査する必要がある。

contractor: 請負業者

363. (C)

そのレストランはわずか6カ月前に建てられたが、かなり古風に見えた。

strikingly: 際立って、著しく

364. (B)

Regent Hotelは、客室の3分の2がオーシャンビューになるように設計されている。

解説

選択肢には接続詞(句)が並んでいる。(D) whileは「～の間に」という意味でもよく使われるが、**361**では2つの状況を対比させる「しかし一方で」という意味で使われている。**363**の(C) although (～にも関わらず)と似ているが、althoughには主節の内容を驚きをもって伝えるという機能がある。

もう1問！

365. Some people can work well with background music, while others need quiet surroundings to ------- .

(A) experience (B) concentrate (C) migrate (D) congratulate

▶▶▶ 解答は178ページ

Unit 7
Set 8

366. Because of the high cost of their products, Zotor Tool Company markets them to ------- professional mechanics rather than amateurs.

367. Board members will be ------- informed if there is any change to the meeting schedule.

368. The design team is ------- confident that the changes to the vehicle will be reviewed positively in the press.

369. The number of new homes being constructed in the area rose ------- after plans for a new school were announced.

問題366～370 Unit 7

(A) fairly
(B) sharply
(C) promptly
(D) exclusively

366. Ⓐ Ⓑ Ⓒ Ⓓ
367. Ⓐ Ⓑ Ⓒ Ⓓ
368. Ⓐ Ⓑ Ⓒ Ⓓ
369. Ⓐ Ⓑ Ⓒ Ⓓ

副詞13

選択肢
....
(A) fairly 　副　かなり、公平に　　　　　(B) sharply 　副　急に

(C) promptly 　副　速やかに、即座に

(D) exclusively 　副　もっぱら、ただ～だけ、独占的に

解答・訳
....
366. (D)

製品の製造コストが高いため、Zotor Tool Companyは、アマチュアではなくもっぱらプロの機械工にそれらを販売している。

367. (C)

会議のスケジュールに変更があった場合、役員会のメンバーに速やかに通知されるだろう。

368. (A)

設計チームは、車両に関する変更がマスコミから好意的な評価を得ることにかなり自信を持っている。

369. (B)

その地域で建設中の新しい家の数は、新しい学校の計画が発表された後、急激に増加した。

解説
....
366に入る(D) exclusiveは「他を一切含めず、もっぱら」という意味。(B) sharply（急に）は「突然に」と「変化の程度が大きい」という両方の意味を含んでいる。**369**のrise sharply（急上昇する）はTOEIC頻出の定型表現だ。

もう1問！
....
370. The design team is fairly ------- that the changes to the vehicle will be reviewed positively in the press.

(A) considerate　(B) stable　(C) confident　(D) accurate

▶▶▶ 解答は178ページ

Unit 7
Set 9

371. After installing the new air conditioning system, the worker ------- the filter cleaning procedure.

372. Camden ------- one of the highest tourist satisfaction ratings last year.

373. Sales of the new toy ------- the manufacturer's predictions, and it had trouble keeping up with demand.

374. The plant manager ------- the new interns to ensure that they worked in accordance with the company safety policy.

(A) oversaw
(B) surpassed
(C) boasted
(D) demonstrated

371. Ⓐ Ⓑ Ⓒ Ⓓ
372. Ⓐ Ⓑ Ⓒ Ⓓ
373. Ⓐ Ⓑ Ⓒ Ⓓ
374. Ⓐ Ⓑ Ⓒ Ⓓ

動詞20

選択肢

(A) oversaw 　動　〜を監督した　　(B) surpassed 　動　〜を上回った

(C) boasted 　動　〜を誇った　　(D) demonstrated 　動　〜を実演した

解答・訳

371. (D)

新しい空調システムを設置した後、作業員はフィルターの清掃手順を実演した。

372. (C)

Camden は昨年、観光客満足度において最高評価を誇った。

373. (B)

新しいおもちゃの販売はメーカーの予測を上回り、彼らは需要に追いつくのに苦労した。

374. (A)

工場長は新しいインターンたちを監督し、彼らが会社の安全方針に従って作業するよう徹底した。

解説

選択肢には動詞の過去形が並んでいる。(A)の oversee は、仕事や活動が正しくなされるように「監督する」という意味で、supervise と同義語だ。(C) boast は、人を主語にして「自慢する、豪語する」という意味で使われるが、**372** のように国や地域を主語にして「〜を誇りにする」という使い方もできる。

もう1問！

375. Camden boasted one of the highest tourist ------- ratings last year.

(A) saturation (B) distraction (C) satisfaction (D) alteration

▶▶▶ 解答は178ページ

Unit 7
Set 10

376. Career Pal helps clients find positions that are both well-paid and ------- .

377. Ms. Kline often takes ------- clients to the assembly plant to show them how carefully our products are made.

378. Public investment has played a ------- role in improving the economy of this region.

379. One more week should be ------- for the construction crew to complete the job on the exterior.

(A) prominent
(B) rewarding
(C) prospective
(D) sufficient

376. Ⓐ Ⓑ Ⓒ Ⓓ
377. Ⓐ Ⓑ Ⓒ Ⓓ
378. Ⓐ Ⓑ Ⓒ Ⓓ
379. Ⓐ Ⓑ Ⓒ Ⓓ

形容詞17

選択肢

(A) prominent　形　目立つ、傑出した　(B) rewarding　形　やりがいのある

(C) prospective　形　見込みのある　　(D) sufficient　形　十分な

解答・訳

376. (B)

Career Palは、クライアントが給料が良く、かつ、やりがいのある職を見つけることを支援している。

377. (C)

Klineさんは見込み客を組み立て工場に度々連れて行き、わが社の製品がどれほど慎重に作られているかを見せている。

378. (A)

公共投資は、この地域の経済を改善する上で際立った役割を果たしてきた。

379. (D)

もう1週間あれば、建設作業員が外装の作業を完了するには十分だ。

解説

(B) rewarding は、何か重要なことや役に立つことをして満足感が得られる、つまり「やりがいのある」という意味。(C) prospective は、語源的には pro（前に）＋spect（見る）で、未来に目にし得る、つまり「見込みのある」となる。**377**の prospective clients（見込み客）という組み合わせを覚えておこう。

もう1問！

380. Public investment has ------- a prominent role in improving the economy of this region.

　　(A) started　(B) given　(C) assigned　(D) played

▶▶▶ 解答は178ページ

174

Unit 7
Set 11

381. Hawkwind's new truck has enough cargo space to ------- most people in the building industry.

382. Upon your arrival, an organizer will ------- you with a handout to help you follow the presentation.

383. LL Intelligence Networks will ------- facial recognition functions into its new line of mobile devices.

384. Max Simms was asked to ------- on the organizing committee for Byron Bay's annual coffee festival.

問題 381~385　Unit 7

(A) provide
(B) serve
(C) introduce
(D) satisfy

381. Ⓐ Ⓑ Ⓒ Ⓓ
382. Ⓐ Ⓑ Ⓒ Ⓓ
383. Ⓐ Ⓑ Ⓒ Ⓓ
384. Ⓐ Ⓑ Ⓒ Ⓓ

動詞21

選択肢

(A) provide 動 ~を提供する　　(B) serve 動 勤める、仕える

(C) introduce 動 ~を導入する　　(D) satisfy 動 ~を満足させる

解答・訳

381. (D)

Hawkwindの新しいトラックには、建築業界のほとんどの人々を満足させるのに十分な貨物スペースがある。

382. (A)

ご到着の際に、プレゼンテーションを理解するのに役立つ資料を主催者からお渡しします。

383. (C)

LL Intelligence Networksは、モバイル機器の新シリーズに顔認識機能を導入する。

384. (B)

Max Simmsは、Byron Bayで毎年開催されているコーヒーフェスティバルの組織委員会の委員を務めるよう依頼された。

解説

382は空所後ろのwithを見た瞬間にprovide A with B（AにBを提供する）という定型表現を想起し即答したいところだ。(B) serveは「飲食物を出す」という意味だけでなく、**384**のように「（企業や組織などで）勤める、仕える、勤務する」という意味でも使われるので要注意。

もう1問！

385. Upon your arrival, an organizer will provide you with a ------- to help you follow the presentation.

　　(A) supervisor　(B) feedback　(C) handout　(D) view

▶▶▶ 解答は178ページ

Unit 7 もう1問！ 解答一覧

※問題文の訳は(→　)内のページ・番号を参照してください

335. (C)

The credit card company recommends that customers check their receipts against their monthly ------- online.

(A) status　　　名 状態　　　　　　(B) purchases　　名 購入
(C) statements　名 収支報告書　　　(D) calculations　名 計算

340. (B)

Accountants at Freeman Associates read all the major industry ------- to ensure that their financial advice is current.

(A) timelines　　名 予定表　　　　(B) journals　　　名 雑誌
(C) standards　　名 基準　　　　　(D) merchandise　名 商品

(→ p. 158、**336**)

345. (A)

The changes to the design will hopefully make the new ------- easier to clean and more dependable.

(A) appliances　名 家電　　　　　(B) operations　　名 操作
(C) signatures　名 署名　　　　　(D) manuscripts　名 原稿

(→ p. 160、**343**)

350. (C)

As the projector was still covered by a warranty, we were able to demand a ------- when it broke down.

(A) reward　　　名 褒賞　　　　　(B) solution　　　名 解決
(C) replacement　名 交換、代替品　(D) deposit　　　名 保証金

(→ p. 162、**346**)

355. (D)

If the storage space is not ------- covered, construction materials may be exposed to bad weather.

(A) closely　　　副 密接に　　　　(B) evenly　　　　副 均等に
(C) exactly　　　副 正確に　　　　(D) securely　　　副 しっかりと

(→ p. 164、**353**)

360. (A)

Before purchase, please check the specifications of your computer to make sure that this device is ------- compatible.

(A) entirely	副 完全に	(B) hardly	副 決して〜ない
(C) environmentally	副 環境的に	(D) genuinely	副 心から

(→ p. 166、**356**)

365. (B)

Some people can work well with background music, while others need quiet surroundings to ------- .

(A) experience	動 経験する	(B) concentrate	動 集中する
(C) migrate	動 移住する	(D) congratulate	動 祝福する

(→ p. 168、**361**)

370. (C)

The design team is fairly ------- that the changes to the vehicle will be reviewed positively in the press.

(A) considerate	形 思いやりのある	(B) stable	形 安定した
(C) confident	形 自信を持った	(D) accurate	形 正確な

(→ p. 170、**368**)

375. (C)

Camden City boasted one of the highest tourist ------- ratings last year.

(A) saturation	名 飽和	(B) distraction	名 気晴らし
(C) satisfaction	名 満足	(D) alteration	名 変更

(→ p. 172、**372**)

380. (D)

Public investment has ------- a prominent role in improving the economy of this region.

(A) started	動 〜を開始した	(B) given	動 〜を与えた
(C) assigned	動 〜を割り当てた	(D) played	動 〜を果たした

(→ p. 174、**378**)

385. (C)

Upon your arrival, an organizer will provide you with a ------- to help you follow the presentation.

(A) supervisor	名 監督者	(B) feedback	名 フィードバック、評価
(C) handout	名 資料	(D) view	名 見解

(→ p. 176、**382**)

Unit 8
Set 1

386. Safety guidelines in the chemical industry have been ------- improved in the last 20 years.

387. Simpson Rental has a wide variety of equipment for rent and can supply ------- anything needed by the construction industry.

388. The cleaners worked ------- to ensure that the display apartment was ready for the inspection.

389. The success of Le Pont Neuf jewelry store is ------- due to its founder, Elle Laroche.

(A) diligently
(B) primarily
(C) virtually
(D) measurably

問題386-390 Unit 8

386. Ⓐ Ⓑ Ⓒ Ⓓ
387. Ⓐ Ⓑ Ⓒ Ⓓ
388. Ⓐ Ⓑ Ⓒ Ⓓ
389. Ⓐ Ⓑ Ⓒ Ⓓ

選択肢

(A) diligently 副 熱心に (B) primarily 副 主に、主として

(C) virtually 副 実質的には (D) measurably 副 かなり

解答・訳

386. (D)

化学業界の安全ガイドラインは、過去20年間でかなり改善されている。

387. (C)

Simpson Rentalは、レンタル用のさまざまな機材を取り揃えており、建設業界で必要とされる物のほぼすべてを実質的に提供できる。

388. (A)

清掃人たちは、展示用のアパートを検査できる状態にするために、熱心に働いた。

389. (B)

Le Pont Neuf宝石店の成功は、主として創業者のElle Larocheによるものだ。

解説

386に入る(D) measurablyは「（測定できて）他の人に明らかに分かるほど」ということから「かなり」という意味になる。**387**に入る(C) virtuallyは「ほとんど同じで、わずかな差が重要ではない状態」を表す際に使われる。**388**のwork diligently（熱心に働く）もTOEIC頻出表現だ。

もう1問！

390. Safety ------- in the chemical industry have been measurably improved in the last 20 years.

　　(A) hazards　(B) guidelines　(C) data　(D) concerns

▶▶▶ 解答は201ページ

Unit 8

Set 2

391. Information about the company's planned purchase of the Dunbar Building should be kept strictly ------- .

392. As the lab technicians perform highly ------- work, it will be hard to find a replacement for Mr. Parnell.

393. Unless otherwise ------- , all rental cars must be returned with a full tank of fuel.

394. Because of an agreement it has with its distributors, Marrakesh Appliances cannot sell ------- units to the public.

(A) specialized
(B) individual
(C) specified
(D) confidential

問題391-395 Unit 8

391. Ⓐ Ⓑ Ⓒ Ⓓ
392. Ⓐ Ⓑ Ⓒ Ⓓ
393. Ⓐ Ⓑ Ⓒ Ⓓ
394. Ⓐ Ⓑ Ⓒ Ⓓ

形容詞18

選択肢

(A) specialized 形 専門化した　　(B) individual 形 個々の
(C) specified 形 指定の、特定の　(D) confidential 形 秘密の、極秘の

解答・訳

391. (D)

会社が計画しているDunbar Buildingの購入に関する情報は、極秘に保管される必要がある。

392. (A)

研究室の技術者が高度に専門化された作業を行うため、Parnellさんに代わる人を見つけるのは難しいだろう。

393. (C)

特に指定のない限り、全てのレンタカーは燃料満タン状態で返却しなければいけない。

394. (B)

販売業者との契約により、Marrakesh Appliancesは個々のユニットを一般向けに販売することはできない。
distributor: 販売業者、卸業者

解説

選択肢には形容詞が並んでいる。**391**のstrictly confidential（極秘の）はTOEIC頻出の定型表現。confidential document（機密文書）のように名詞の前に置かれることもある。**394**のunless otherwise specifiedは「特に指定のない限り」という意味の表現で、これもよく使われる。

もう1問！

395. Unless otherwise specified, all rental cars must be returned with a
full tank of ------- .

(A) fuel　(B) beak　(C) aid　(D) energy

▶▶▶ 解答は201ページ

Unit 8

Set 3

396. Environmental activists ------- the use of plastic shopping bags and suggest using more eco-friendly alternatives.

397. To compete effectively, companies try to ------- what trends in technology will benefit them.

398. The LifeSpark Group sent a letter to all customers to ------- purchasing travel insurance before their trip abroad.

399. Most antivirus software providers ------- on releasing updates frequently to combat security risks.

(A) predict
(B) insist
(C) oppose
(D) recommend

396. Ⓐ Ⓑ Ⓒ Ⓓ
397. Ⓐ Ⓑ Ⓒ Ⓓ
398. Ⓐ Ⓑ Ⓒ Ⓓ
399. Ⓐ Ⓑ Ⓒ Ⓓ

動詞22

(A) predict 動 〜を予測する　　(B) insist 動 主張する、強く求める

(C) oppose 動 〜に反対する　　(D) recommend 動 〜を勧める

正解・訳

396. (C)

環境保護活動家はプラスチック製買い物袋の使用に反対し、より環境に優しい代替品を使うことを提案している。

397. (A)

より効率的に競争するために、企業はどのようなテクノロジーの最新傾向が自社に利益をもたらすかを予測しようとする。

398. (D)

LifeSpark Group は海外旅行の前に旅行保険に加入するよう勧めるために全ての顧客に手紙を出した。

purchase an insurance: 保険に加入する

399. (B)

多くのアンチウイルスソフトウェアのサービス事業者はセキュリティーの危機に対抗するため、アップデートを頻繁に公開することを主張する。

解説

(C) oppose は他動詞で「〜に反対する」。be opposed to 〜 という形で使われることも多い。397に入る (A) predict (予言する) は pre (前もって) dict (言う) という接頭辞＋語根で覚えておこう。398 は空所後の on がヒントだ。insist on 〜 (〜を主張する) のように、前置詞と一緒に覚えておくと即答できる。

もう1問！

400. To compete effectively, companies try to predict what trends in technology will ------- them.

(A) possess　(B) hold　(C) enforce　(D) benefit

▶▶▶ 解答は201ページ

Unit 8
Set 4

401. Due to a change in company procedures, more
------- are available to hard-working employees.

402. After failing to meet the safety ------- of the Ministry
of Health, some restaurants have been closed until
further notice.

403. Written ------- were required in order to make the
contracts between the two parties legally binding.

404. Before publishing a project report, please make
sure that it includes a page of ------- to thank your
collaborators.

(A) requirements
(B) acknowledgments
(C) benefits
(D) agreements

問題401-405 Unit 8

401. Ⓐ Ⓑ Ⓒ Ⓓ
402. Ⓐ Ⓑ Ⓒ Ⓓ
403. Ⓐ Ⓑ Ⓒ Ⓓ
404. Ⓐ Ⓑ Ⓒ Ⓓ

名詞18

選択肢

(A) requirements [名] 要件、必要条件　(B) acknowledgements [名] (著者の) 謝辞
(C) benefits [名] 手当、給付金　(D) agreements [名] 契約、協定

解答・訳

401. (C)

社内手続きが変更されたため、勤勉な社員はより多くの**手当**を得ることができる。

402. (A)

保健省の安全**基準**を満たせなかった後、一部のレストランは追って通知があるまで営業をやめている。

403. (D)

二者間の契約に法的な拘束力を持たせるため、書面による**契約**が必要だった。
binding: 拘束力のある、義務的な

404. (B)

プロジェクト報告書を発表する前に、それに協力者に感謝するための**謝辞**のページが含まれていることを確認してください。
collaborator: 協力者、共同研究者

解説

benefit (利益) は **401** のように「手当」という意味で使う場合、benefits と複数形になる。**402** の動詞 meet (～を満たす) は requirements (要件) や demands (需要) などと共によく使われる。**403** の written agreements とは「契約書」のこと。(B) の acknowledgements は **404** の文脈では著者の「謝辞」。他に「受領通知」という意味もある。

もう1問！

405. After failing to meet the safety requirements of the Ministry of Health, some restaurants have been closed until further ------- .

(A) notice　(B) submission　(C) entrance　(D) interruption

▶▶▶ 解答は201ページ

Unit 8
Set 5

406. Mr. Daniels gave project managers a ------- presentation on the importance of submitting weekly progress reports.

407. Devon James' daily sports show attracts a ------- audience of listeners from around the world.

408. The owner of the building has lowered the rent because it has been ------- for almost a year.

409. Tanya Wood moved from a ------- location to the metropolitan area to find a job with a higher salary.

(A) vacant
(B) sizable
(C) persuasive
(D) rural

問題406~410 Unit 8

406. Ⓐ Ⓑ Ⓒ Ⓓ
407. Ⓐ Ⓑ Ⓒ Ⓓ
408. Ⓐ Ⓑ Ⓒ Ⓓ
409. Ⓐ Ⓑ Ⓒ Ⓓ

形容詞19

選択肢

(A) vacant 形 空の   (B) sizable 形 かなり大きな、かなり多くの
(C) persuasive 形 説得力のある   (D) rural 形 地方の、田舎の

解答・訳

406. (C)

Danielsさんはプロジェクトマネージャーたちに対し、1週間ごとの進捗レポートを提出する重要性について<u>説得力のある</u>プレゼンテーションを行った。

407. (B)

Devon Jamesの毎日のスポーツ番組は、世界中の<u>大勢の</u>聴衆を魅了している。

408. (A)

建物の所有者は、それが1年近く<u>空室</u>だったため、家賃を引き下げた。

409. (D)

Tanya Woodは、より高い給料の仕事を見つけるために、<u>地方</u>から大都市圏に引っ越した。

解説

選択肢には形容詞が並んでいる。(C) persuasive は「何かを信じさせ、行動を促すような」というニュアンス。**406**のpersuasive presentation（説得力のあるプレゼン）はよく使われる定型表現だ。(B) sizable は fairly large（かなり大きい）と同義。サイズを計れるといった意味は一切ないので要注意。

もう1問！

410. The owner of the building has ------- the rent because it has been vacant for almost a year.

(A) admitted (B) returned (C) paid (D) lowered

▶▶▶ 解答は201ページ

Unit 8
Set 6

411. Mr. Stanton agreed to meet with representatives of a textile factory ------- his trip to Mumbai.

412. Mr. Rylands worked as a staff writer at *Whitman Times* ------- four years before he was offered the editor position.

413. Let's wait ------- the revised building proposal has been issued before we make any decisions.

414. Employees are expected to submit expense reports ------- a week of their return from business trips.

(A) until
(B) within
(C) during
(D) for

問題411〜415 Unit 8

411. Ⓐ Ⓑ Ⓒ Ⓓ
412. Ⓐ Ⓑ Ⓒ Ⓓ
413. Ⓐ Ⓑ Ⓒ Ⓓ
414. Ⓐ Ⓑ Ⓒ Ⓓ

前置詞05

選択肢

(A) until　前 ～まで　　(B) within　前 ～以内
(C) during　前 ～の間に　　(D) for　前 ～の間

正解・訳

411. (C)
Stanton さんは Mumbai への出張の間に織物工場の代表者と会うことに同意した。
textile: 織物

412. (D)
Rylands さんは編集者の職をオファーされるまでの4年の間、*Whitman Times* でスタッフライターとして働いていた。

413. (A)
何らかの決定を下すのは、修正された建築案が発表されるまで待ちましょう。

414. (B)
社員は出張から戻って1週間以内に旅行の経費報告書を提出することになっている。
be expected to do: ～することになっている

解説

(C) during と (D) for は両方とも「～の間」と訳されるが、用法は異なる。**411** の trip（出張）のような特定の期間の前では during を、**412** の数字を含む表現の前では for を用いる。**413** の wait until ~（～まで待つ）は定番の表現。**414** の within one week（1週間以内）は、in one week（1週間後）との使い分けに注意したい。

もう1問！

415. Let's wait until the revised building proposal has been ------- before we make any decisions.

(A) postponed　(B) issued　(C) fostered　(D) exceeded

▶▶▶ 解答は202ページ

Unit 8

Set 7

416. Mr. Fredricks paid for ------- shipping to ensure that his computer equipment would arrive on time.

417. Some tour operators avoid using Grendel Hotel because it charges extra for ------- check-ins.

418. Mr. Zhou's marketing poster was ------- what the advertising department requested for the next campaign.

419. Due to shrinking domestic market for its products, DeLight Games is now seeking to expand its business ------- .

(A) overnight
(B) abroad
(C) late
(D) exactly

問題416~420 Unit 8

416. Ⓐ Ⓑ Ⓒ Ⓓ
417. Ⓐ Ⓑ Ⓒ Ⓓ
418. Ⓐ Ⓑ Ⓒ Ⓓ
419. Ⓐ Ⓑ Ⓒ Ⓓ

形容詞・副詞

選択肢

(A) overnight 形 翌日の、1泊の 副 一晩中　(B) abroad 副 国外に、海外へ
(C) late 形 遅い 副 遅れて　　　　　　　　(D) exactly 副 まさに、正確に

正解・訳

416. (A)

Fredricks さんはコンピューター機器が予定通りに届くよう、翌日配達便の料金を支払った。

417. (C)

Grandel Hotel は遅い時間にチェックインすると追加料金を課すため、避ける旅行業者もある。

418. (D)

Zhou さんの宣伝ポスターは、まさに宣伝部が次のキャンペーンのために依頼した通りのものだった。

419. (B)

製品の国内市場が縮小したため、DeLight Games はビジネスを国外に拡大しようとしている。

domestic: 国内の／seek: 〜しようとする

解説

416 は、overnight shipping（翌日配達）という連語だと気付くことができれば即答できる。(D)の exactly は what 節を伴い「まさに…なもの」という意味で、**418** では「まさに要求されていたもの」となる。**419**の(B) abroad は expand（拡大する）という動詞を修飾している。副詞なので、business to abroad とはならない点に注意。

もう1問！

420. Some tour operators ------- using Grendel Hotel because it charges extra for late check-ins.

(A) prefer　(B) admit　(C) avoid　(D) suggest

▶▶▶ 解答は202ページ

Unit 8

Set 8

421. It is necessary to obtain ------- from a section manager before using any of the company vehicles.

422. At her retirement party, Ms. Tanner received ------- for her years of hard work.

423. One of our representatives will perform a free ------- of your office's cleaning needs and provide an instant quote.

424. Please contact the town planning department if you need ------- of any of the city's construction regulations.

(A) recognition
(B) permission
(C) assessment
(D) clarification

問題421～425 Unit 8

421. Ⓐ Ⓑ Ⓒ Ⓓ
422. Ⓐ Ⓑ Ⓒ Ⓓ
423. Ⓐ Ⓑ Ⓒ Ⓓ
424. Ⓐ Ⓑ Ⓒ Ⓓ

名詞19

選択肢

....

(A) recognition 名 （功績を）認めること、表彰

(B) permission 名 承諾、許可

(C) assessment 名 査定、評価 (D) clarification 名 説明、明確化

正解・訳

....

421. (B)

社用車を利用する際は、課長から事前に許可を得る必要がある。

422. (A)

退職パーティーにて、Tannerさんは長年の功績に対する表彰を受けた。
retirement: 退職

423. (C)

当社の担当者が、お客様のオフィスの清掃業務について無料の査定を実施し、すぐに見積もりを提供いたします。

424. (D)

市の建築基準について何か説明が必要な場合は、都市計画部にご連絡ください。

解説

....

421、社用車の使用前に得る必要があるのは(B) permission (許可)。問題文では前置詞fromとともに用いられ「どこから」その許可を得るのかにも言及することが多い。**422**は空所の後に「長年の功績に対して」と続くことから(A) recognition (表彰) が正解。**423**は見積もり前に行われることを考えると(C) assessment (査定) が妥当だ。

もう1問！

....

425. One of our representatives will perform a free assessment of your office's cleaning needs and provide an ------- quote.

(A) infinite (B) extra (C) instant (D) unlimited

▶▶▶ 解答は202ページ

Unit 8

Set 9

426. Because the new printing equipment is faster and cheaper to run, we now print company brochures more ------- .

427. Many customers commented on how prices had risen ------- over the last six months.

428. Shipping your packages with Media Mailer is simple because our system will ------- print out postage and shipping labels.

429. Be sure to estimate your annual car mileage as ------- as possible when obtaining a car insurance quote.

(A) automatically
(B) efficiently
(C) dramatically
(D) accurately

426. Ⓐ Ⓑ Ⓒ Ⓓ
427. Ⓐ Ⓑ Ⓒ Ⓓ
428. Ⓐ Ⓑ Ⓒ Ⓓ
429. Ⓐ Ⓑ Ⓒ Ⓓ

選択肢

(A) automatically 副 自動で (B) efficiently 副 効率的に

(C) dramatically 副 著しく、劇的に (D) accurately 副 正確に

正解・訳

426. (B)

新しい印刷機器は動作がより速く運用経費も安いため、会社のパンフレットをより効率的に印刷できる。

brochure: パンフレット

427. (C)

過去6カ月の間にいかに著しく物価が上昇したかについて、多くの顧客が意見を述べた。

428. (A)

システムが自動的に切手と宛名ラベルを印刷するため、Media Mailer を使って荷物を送ることは簡単です。

429. (D)

自動車保険の保険料の見積もりを請求する際には、年間走行距離を可能な限り正確に推定するようにしてください。

解説

426 は前半の faster and cheaper（より速くて安い）を言い換えた (B) efficiently が適切。(C) の dramatically（劇的に、著しく）は **427** のような増減や変化を表す動詞を修飾する。drastically とは類義語だ。**429** は空所後の動詞 estimate（〜を推測する）と相性が良い (D) accurately を選ぶ。類義語は correctly だが、accurately には「注意を払って正確を期す」という意味合いがある。

もう1問！

430. Be sure to estimate your annual car mileage as accurately as possible when obtaining a car insurance ------- .

(A) quote (B) certificate (C) policy (D) premium

▶▶▶ 解答は202ページ

Unit 8

Set 10

431. GTC Inc. has generously agreed to ------- 5 percent of its profits to environmental causes this year.

432. The company owners ------- that their initial success was a result of good luck rather than clever planning.

433. Inserting flyers in the local newspaper is an effective way to ------- your business.

434. The Bridgewater coffee maker allows users to ------- the settings to their personal preferences.

(A) admit
(B) allocate
(C) adjust
(D) advertise

問題 431~435　Unit 8

431. Ⓐ Ⓑ Ⓒ Ⓓ
432. Ⓐ Ⓑ Ⓒ Ⓓ
433. Ⓐ Ⓑ Ⓒ Ⓓ
434. Ⓐ Ⓑ Ⓒ Ⓓ

動詞23

選択肢

(A) admit 動 ～を認める   (B) allocate 動 ～を割り当てる

(C) adjust 動 ～を調節する   (D) advertise 動 ～を宣伝する

正解・訳

431. (B)

GTC社は今年、収益の5パーセントを環境保護運動に割り当てることに寛大に同意した。

432. (A)

会社の経営者たちは、自分たちの最初の成功は賢明な計画によるものではなく、運が良かったおかげだと認める。
initial: 初めの／clever: 賢い

433. (D)

地元の新聞にちらしを折り込むことは企業を宣伝するための効果的な方法だ。

434. (C)

Bridgewaterのコーヒーメーカーは、設定を個人的な好みに調節することが可能だ。

解説

431の空所に入る動詞の目的語はprofits（利益）。利益を「環境保護運動」に対してどうするかを考えると、(B) allocate（～を割り当てる）が適切。allocate A to B（AをBに割り当てる）で覚えよう。**433**と**434**も動詞の後の語（「宣伝する」「調節する」対象）との相性で解く。**432**は動詞の後にthat節が取れる(A) admitが正解。admit that S＋Vで「SがVすることを認める」となる。

もう1問！

435. GTC Inc. has generously agreed to allocate 5 percent of its profits to environmental ------- this year.

(A) causes (B) reasons (C) arguments (D) resources

▶▶▶ 解答は202ページ

Unit 8

Set 11

436. With a seating -------- of up to 350 guests, the Brown Hall is the perfect venue for corporate events and private parties.

437. With the construction deadline drawing near, the company president asked for a ------- report.

438. After it was found that the plant's running costs had increased, managers discussed ways of improving ------- .

439. The designers of the T56 digital camera felt that a wireless Internet connection would be an important ------- .

(A) capacity
(B) efficiency
(C) progress
(D) function

問題 436~440 Unit 8

436. Ⓐ Ⓑ Ⓒ Ⓓ
437. Ⓐ Ⓑ Ⓒ Ⓓ
438. Ⓐ Ⓑ Ⓒ Ⓓ
439. Ⓐ Ⓑ Ⓒ Ⓓ

名詞20

選択肢

(A) capacity 名 収容能力、能力　(B) efficiency 名 効率、効率性

(C) progress 名 進展、進捗　(D) function 名 機能

正解・訳

436. (A)

Brown Hallには350人までの収容能力があり、会社の催しや私的なパーティーに最適な会場だ。

437. (C)

建設期限が徐々に近付いていることに伴い、社長は進捗報告書を求めた。
draw near: だんだんと近づく

438. (B)

工場の運転経費の上昇が発覚した後、部長たちは効率性の改善方法について話し合った。

439. (D)

T56デジタルカメラの設計者たちは、無線インターネット接続こそが重要な機能となるだろうと考えた。

解説

436、seating（座席の）の後ろに入り得るのは(A)のcapacity（収容力）のみだ。seating capacityで「座席数、定員」となる。**438**、「維持費の上昇」への対策としてはimprove efficiency（効率性の改善）が考えられる。**437**のprogress report（進捗報告書）はそのまま覚えておこう。

もう1問！

440. With the construction deadline ------- near, the company president asked for a progress report.

　　(A) yielding　(B) drawing　(C) streaming　(D) presenting

▶▶▶ 解答は202ページ

Unit 8 もう1問！解答一覧

※問題文の訳は(→　)内のページ・番号を参照してください

390. (B)

Safety ------- in the chemical industry have been measurably improved in the last 20 years.

(A) hazards 名 危険要因 (B) guidelines 名 ガイドライン、指針
(C) data 名 データ (D) concerns 名 懸念

(→ p. 180、**386**)

395. (A)

Unless otherwise specified, all rental cars must be returned with a full tank of ------- .

(A) fuel 名 燃料 (B) beak 名 くちばし
(C) aid 名 援助 (D) energy 名 エネルギー

(→ p. 182、**393**)

400. (D)

To compete effectively, companies try to predict what trends in technology will ------- them.

(A) possess 動 ～を所有する (B) hold 動 ～を持つ
(C) enforce 動 ～を強化する、 (D) benefit 動 ～の利益になる
　　　　　　　　～を施行する

(→ p. 184、**397**)

405. (A)

After failing to meet the safety requirements of the Ministry of Health, some restaurants have been closed until further -------.

(A) notice 名 通知 (B) submission 名 提出
(C) entrance 名 入り口 (D) interruption 名 中断

(→ p. 186、**402**)

410. (D)

The owner of the building has ------- the rent because it has been vacant for almost a year.

(A) admitted 動 ～を認めた (B) returned 動 ～を返した
(C) paid 動 ～を支払った (D) lowered 動 ～を下げた

(→ p. 188、**408**)

415. (B)

Let's wait until the revised building proposal has been ------- before we make any decisions.

(A) postponed 　動 ～を延期した　　(B) issued 　動 ～を発行した
(C) fostered 　動 ～を発展させた　　(D) exceeded 　動 ～を超えた

420. (C)

Some tour operators ------- using Grendel Hotel because it charges extra for late check-ins.

(A) prefer 　動 ～を好む　　(B) admit 　動 ～を認める
(C) avoid 　動 ～を避ける　　(D) suggest 　動 ～を提案する

(→ p. 192、417)

425. (C)

One of our representatives will perform a free assessment of your office's cleaning needs and provide an ------- quote.

(A) infinite 　形 無限の　　(B) extra 　形 追加の
(C) instant 　形 即時の　　(D) unlimited 　形 無制限の

(→ p. 194、423)

430. (A)

Be sure to estimate your annual car mileage as accurately as possible when obtaining a car insurance ------- .

(A) quote 　名 見積もり　　(B) certificate 　名 証明書
(C) policy 　名 (保険の) 証書　　(D) premium 　名 保険料

(→ p. 196、429)

435. (A)

GTC Inc. has generously agreed to allocate 5 percent of its profits to environmental ------- this year.

(A) causes 　名 目標、理念　　(B) reasons 　名 理由
(C) arguments 　名 議論、論拠　　(D) resources 　名 資源

(→ p. 198、431)

440. (B)

With the construction deadline ------- near, the company president asked for a progress report.

(A) yielding 　動 生み出している　　(B) drawing 　動 近づいている
(C) streaming 　動 流れている　　(D) presenting 　動 提示している、見せている

(→ p. 200、437)

Unit 9

Set 1

441. Although *Commodus* performed very well among young audiences, many film critics thought its script was ------- compelling nor sophisticated.

442. The latest novel of award-winning author Yoko Chambers is available ------- in Japanese and in English.

443. Attendees of the company retreat can choose to go ------- by bus or private vehicle.

444. Kelli Peters is ------- a best-selling novelist but also an award-winning journalist.

    (A) either
    (B) not only
    (C) both
    (D) neither

問題441~445 Unit 9

441. Ⓐ Ⓑ Ⓒ Ⓓ
442. Ⓐ Ⓑ Ⓒ Ⓓ
443. Ⓐ Ⓑ Ⓒ Ⓓ
444. Ⓐ Ⓑ Ⓒ Ⓓ

選択肢

(A) either 接代 ～のどちらか   (B) not only ～だけではなく

(C) both 形代 2つとも、どちらも   (D) neither 接代 どちらも～でない

正解・訳

441. (D)

*Commodus*は若い観客には好評だったが、多くの映画評論家はその脚本が魅力的でもなく洗練されてもいないと感じた。

442. (C)

受賞作家Yoko Chambersの最新の小説は、日本語版と英語版のどちらも入手できる。

443. (A)

社員旅行の参加者は、バスと自家用車のどちらで行くかを選ぶことができる。

company retreat:（研修などを兼ねて行われる）社員旅行

444. (B)

Kelli Petersはベストセラー作家であるだけではなく、受賞歴のあるジャーナリストでもある。

解説

接続詞（句）とセットで使われる語句が並んでいる。**441**はneither A nor B（AもBも～でない）、**442**はboth A and B（AとBの両方）、**443**はeither A or B（AとBのどちらか）、**444**はnot only A but also B（AだけではなくBも）という定型表現を見抜けるかが鍵。なお、alsoが省略されてnot only A but Bとなることも多い。

もう1問！

445. Although *Commodus* performed very well among young audiences, many film critics thought its script was neither ------- nor sophisticated.

(A) compelling (B) obsolete (C) unbelievable (D) ample

▶▶▶ 解答は225ページ

Unit 9

Set 2

446. Ms. Arista was appointed manager of the Madrid branch because of her ------- knowledge of Spanish language and culture.

447. Employees at Highwood Green Tech are encouraged to ride their bicycles to work whenever ------- .

448. The salary offered to the successful candidate will be ------- to his or her experience.

449. Employees may use cheaper services as long as the quality is ------- to that of the companies we usually rely on.

(A) equivalent
(B) proportional
(C) extensive
(D) possible

446. Ⓐ Ⓑ Ⓒ Ⓓ
447. Ⓐ Ⓑ Ⓒ Ⓓ
448. Ⓐ Ⓑ Ⓒ Ⓓ
449. Ⓐ Ⓑ Ⓒ Ⓓ

形容詞20

選択肢

(A) equivalent [形] 同等の   (B) proportional [形] 比例した

(C) extensive [形] 広範囲の、幅広い   (D) possible [形] 可能な

正解・訳

446. (C)

Aristaさんは、スペインの言語や文化に関して幅広い知識を持っているため、Madrid支店の支店長に任命された。

447. (D)

Highwood Green Techの従業員は、可能なときは常に自転車で通勤するよう奨励されている。

448. (B)

採用される候補者への月給は、その人の経験に比例したものとなる。

449. (A)

わが社が普段利用している会社のものと質が同等である限り、従業員はより安価なサービスを利用してもよい。

as long as ~: 〜である限り

解説

(C) extensive は「空間の広さ」に限らず、446のknowledgeやresearchなどの語を形容して「量の多さ、深さ」を表すこともできる。448の(B) proportional（比例した）と449の(A) equivalent（同等の）は、何かと比較した上で使われる単語なので、比較対象とつなげる前置詞toとともに覚えよう。448では月給と経験を、449では2つのサービスの質を比較している。

もう1問！

450. Ms. Arista was ------- manager of the Madrid branch because of her extensive knowledge of Spanish language and culture.

     (A) consulted   (B) achieved   (C) proposed   (D) appointed

▶▶▶ 解答は225ページ

Unit 9
Set 3

451. To expedite inquiries when contacting the Esteem Bank, clients must provide a ------- code.

452. If you are not home to receive your delivery, the driver will leave a card with a ------- number.

453. In order to strengthen its ------- with its most valued client, Steadwell Industries sends representatives to Chicago several times a year.

454. Career guidance classes at Greensborough Community College are free, but it is necessary to register in ------- .

(A) reference
(B) relationship
(C) contact
(D) advance

問題451~455 Unit 9

451. Ⓐ Ⓑ Ⓒ Ⓓ
452. Ⓐ Ⓑ Ⓒ Ⓓ
453. Ⓐ Ⓑ Ⓒ Ⓓ
454. Ⓐ Ⓑ Ⓒ Ⓓ

名詞21

選択肢
....
(A) reference　名（顧客や手紙などの）参照（整理）番号　(B) relationship　名 関係
(C) contact　名形 連絡先（の）　(D) advance　名 前進、（in advance で）事前

正解・訳
....

451. (A)

Esteem銀行へ連絡する際、問い合わせを効率よく進めるために、顧客は参照コードを
知らせなければならない。
expedite: 〜を早める

452. (C)

ご自宅に不在で荷物をお受け取りになれない場合、配達員が連絡先の電話番号を記し
たカードを残します。

453. (B)

大切な顧客との関係を強化するため、Steadwell Industries は担当者を年に数回、Chicago
に派遣している。
strengthen: 〜を強化する

454. (D)

Greensborough Community Collegeの職業指導の授業は無料だが、事前の登録が必要で
ある。

解説
....
451のreference code（参照コード）は、サービスなどを受ける際に提示する整理番号。
フレーズで覚えておこう。**452**の空所には、荷物を受け取るのに必要となる配達員の
「連絡」先が入ると推測できる。**454**のin advance（事前に）は頻出フレーズ。強調する
ときは前にwellを足してwell in advance（余裕を持って）という形で使う。

もう1問！
....
455. In order to strengthen its relationship with its most ------- client,
　　　　Steadwell Industries sends representatives to Chicago several
　　　　times a year.

　　　　(A) variable　(B) perceptive　(C) valued　(D) premiered

▶▶▶ 解答は225ページ

Unit 9

Set 4

456. Our offices have been ------- relocated to the Oxford Pines Mall due to the renovation.

457. The advisory board meetings typically take two hours but can ------- last much longer.

458. The high-speed train ride from Paris to London takes ------- two and a half hours.

459. Livida Beauty Products is ------- in merger talks with an online cosmetics retailer in hopes of expanding its customer base.

(A) approximately
(B) reportedly
(C) occasionally
(D) temporarily

456. Ⓐ Ⓑ Ⓒ Ⓓ
457. Ⓐ Ⓑ Ⓒ Ⓓ
458. Ⓐ Ⓑ Ⓒ Ⓓ
459. Ⓐ Ⓑ Ⓒ Ⓓ

選択肢

(A) approximately 副 およそ　　(B) reportedly 副 伝えられるところによると

(C) occasionally 副 時々　　(D) temporarily 副 一時的に

正解・訳

456. (D)

改修工事のため、弊社のオフィスは<u>一時的に</u>Oxford Pines Mallに移転しています。

457. (C)

通常ならば諮問委員会は2時間だが、<u>時々</u>それよりもずっと長く続くことがある。
typically: 通常は

458. (A)

ParisからLondonへは高速列車に乗って<u>およそ</u>2時間半かかる。
ride:（乗り物に）乗っている時間

459. (B)

<u>伝えられるところによると</u>、Livida Beauty Productsは顧客基盤の拡大を狙って、オンラインの化粧品小売会社と合併交渉中である。
merger talks: 合併交渉

解説

456の後半から移転は改装中に限られた措置だとわかるため、(D)のtemporarily（一時的に）が適切。**457**は、butの前に副詞typically（通常は）があるので、対照的な意味の(D) occasionally（時々）を空所に入れる。**458**は空所後のtwo and a half hoursという数字を含む表現に着目し、(A) approximatelyを選ぶ。roughlyやaroundはその類義語だ。

もう1問！

460. Livida Beauty Products is reportedly in merger talks with an online cosmetics retailer in ------- of expanding its customer base.

(A) cases　(B) hopes　(C) terms　(D) charges

▶▶▶ 解答は225ページ

Unit 9

Set 5

461. Mr. Barton ------- the damaged shipment from the manufacturer and returned it to the factory.

462. The local newspaper reports that the old municipal building will be ------- to construct a new one.

463. Unfavorable weather conditions briefly ------- the construction of the new parking garage.

464. Entry to the worksite is ------- unless you are accompanied by a member of the site management team.

(A) demolished
(B) rejected
(C) prohibited
(D) interrupted

問題 461～465 Unit **9**

461. Ⓐ Ⓑ Ⓒ Ⓓ
462. Ⓐ Ⓑ Ⓒ Ⓓ
463. Ⓐ Ⓑ Ⓒ Ⓓ
464. Ⓐ Ⓑ Ⓒ Ⓓ

動詞24

選択肢

(A) demolished [動] 解体した・された (B) rejected [動] 〜を拒否した・された

(C) prohibited [動] 禁止した・された

(D) interrupted [動] 〜を中断した・された

正解・訳

461. (B)

Bartonさんは、製造者からの破損した荷物を<u>拒否</u>し、工場へ返品した。

462. (A)

地元の新聞紙は、古い市の建物が<u>解体</u>されて、新しいものが建設されると報じている。

municipal: 自治体の、市の

463. (D)

天候状態が望ましくなかったため、新しい車庫の建設が一時的に<u>中断</u>された。

briefly: 一時的に

464. (C)

現場運営チームのメンバーによる同行がない限り、作業現場への立ち入りは<u>禁じられ</u>ています。

accompany: 〜に同行する

解説

動詞の過去形、過去分詞が並んでいる。(B)(C)(D)は行動を止める意味を持つ動詞なので、動作をする人・物と、止められる行動から、空所に入るものを判断する。**461**は主語のMr. Bartonが荷物を拒否し、**463**は天候によって建設が中断している。**464**は現場への立ち入りを禁止している。**462**は建物が主語で、空所の後に「新しい建物に」と続くことから、建て直しの話だと推測できる。

もう1問！

465. Entry to the worksite is prohibited unless you are ------- by a member of the site management team.

(A) anticipated (B) affiliated (C) amended (D) accompanied

▶▶▶ 解答は225ページ

Unit 9

Set 6

466. Most of the employees at Carterware use ------- transportation to get to work.

467. As the factory does not have facilities for food preparation, it relies on ------- sources to supply its cafeteria.

468. In recent years, there has been a significant increase in the number of ------- workers in Japan.

469. *Finance Now* is a monthly magazine that focuses on ------- economic news, including issues in Australia.

(A) outside
(B) foreign
(C) global
(D) public

466. Ⓐ Ⓑ Ⓒ Ⓓ
467. Ⓐ Ⓑ Ⓒ Ⓓ
468. Ⓐ Ⓑ Ⓒ Ⓓ
469. Ⓐ Ⓑ Ⓒ Ⓓ

選択肢

(A) outside 形 外部の　　　　　(B) foreign 形 外国にある

(C) global 形 世界の　　　　　　(D) public 形 公共の

正解・訳

466. (D)

Carterwareの従業員のほとんどが通勤に公共の交通機関を利用している。

work: 仕事、職場　※get to workで「通勤する」。

467. (A)

その工場には食品調理設備がないため、食堂への供給は外部の供給源に頼っている。

468. (B)

この数年で、日本の外国人労働者の数は大幅に増加した。

469. (C)

*Finance Now*は、オーストラリアの問題を含む、世界経済に関するニュースを主に取り上げている月刊誌である。

解説

選択肢に並ぶ単語は「外の世界」に関連した形容詞。**466**のpublic transportationや**468**のforeign countriesのように相性のいい語句とセットで覚えておくことで、解答のスピードアップが可能だ。(A)のoutsideには「屋外の」という意味もあるが、**467**のように「(組織などの) 外部の」という意味で使うこともできる。

もう1問！

470. In ------- years, there has been a significant increase in the number of foreign workers in Japan.

　　　(A) last　(B) multiple　(C) recent　(D) numerous

▶▶▶ 解答は226ページ

Unit 9
Set 7

471. Due to a time ------- , Mr. Thomson had to cut his presentation short.

472. Please obtain ------- from a section manager before taking any office equipment on business trips.

473. The County Health Department will send inspectors to food establishments to confirm their ------- with local regulations.

474. After careful ------- , Hartmann Inc. has decided not to invest in the biotech startup.

    (A) compliance
    (B) constraint
    (C) consideration
    (D) consent

問題471~475　Unit 9

471. Ⓐ Ⓑ Ⓒ Ⓓ
472. Ⓐ Ⓑ Ⓒ Ⓓ
473. Ⓐ Ⓑ Ⓒ Ⓓ
474. Ⓐ Ⓑ Ⓒ Ⓓ

選択肢

(A) compliance 名 遵守

(B) constraint 名 制約

(C) consideration 名 考慮

(D) consent 名 承諾、同意

正解・訳

471. (B)

時間の制約があったため、Thomson さんは発表を短縮しなければならなかった。

472. (D)

出張で会社の備品を持ち出す際には、事前に課長の承諾を得てください。

473. (A)

郡の保健局は検査員を飲食施設に派遣し、地域の条例の遵守を確認する。

474. (C)

Hartmann は、慎重な考慮の末、その生命工学のスタートアップ企業には投資しないと決断した。

startup: スタートアップ企業 ※創業から間もない企業

解説

471 は後半で発表時間を短くする必要があったことを述べているので、時間に「制約」があったと判断できる。due to a time constraint というセットフレーズとして丸ごと覚えよう。**472** は上司から得るものということで(D) consent（同意）を選ぶ。**474** の(C) consideration は「熟考」の意味を持つが、形容詞careful（慎重な）でより強調されている。

もう1問！

475. The County Health Department will send inspectors to food ------- to confirm their compliance with local regulations.

    (A) lines (B) expenditures (C) locations (D) establishments

▶▶▶ 解答は226ページ

Unit 9

Set 8

476. Management hopes that its new financial incentives will ------- employees to work more effectively.

477. Ms. Ames was asked to ------- a speech on the advantages of flexible work hours.

478. Passengers from Chicago were directed to ------- their checked baggage at Carousel 4.

479. By using local ingredients, the company helps ------- the local economy.

(A) deliver
(B) encourage
(C) claim
(D) sustain

問題476-480 Unit 9

476. Ⓐ Ⓑ Ⓒ Ⓓ
477. Ⓐ Ⓑ Ⓒ Ⓓ
478. Ⓐ Ⓑ Ⓒ Ⓓ
479. Ⓐ Ⓑ Ⓒ Ⓓ

選択肢

(A) deliver 動 ～（考えなど）を述べる、～（演説）をする

(B) encourage 動 ～するよう促す

(C) claim 動 ～を引き取る　　(D) sustain 動 ～を維持する

正解・訳

476. (B)

経営陣は、新しい報奨金制度が、従業員のより効率的な労働を促すことを望んでいる。
incentive: 報奨金

477. (A)

Ames さんはフレックスタイム制の利点についてスピーチをするよう依頼された。

478. (C)

Chicago からの乗客は、預けた荷物を4番の回転台で引き取るよう指示された。
carousel:（空港などの）手荷物回転台

479. (D)

その企業は地元の食材を使用することによって、地域経済を維持することに貢献している。

解説

476 は後ろに＜人＞ to do を続けることができる (B) encourage が正解。477 の deliver a speech（スピーチをする）や 478 の claim baggage（荷物を引き取る）も、動詞単独ではなくこのフレーズのまま覚えておくとよい。(C) claim は「～を主張する」という意味でも頻繁に使われる重要語だ。

もう1問！

480. By using local ------- , the company helps sustain the local economy.

(A) recipients　(B) participants　(C) ingredients　(D) components

▶▶▶ 解答は226ページ

Unit 9
Set 9

481. The recent songs by composer Davi Morelli are ------- different from the ones he made before.

482. Bisjobs.com will notify you ------- if any suitable positions are posted by potential employers.

483. The operating manual was ------- only written in English, but now it is available in 10 languages.

484. The TV drama series was canceled ------- at the beginning of its second season due to its low ratings.

(A) initially
(B) abruptly
(C) instantly
(D) utterly

問題481~485 Unit 9

481. Ⓐ Ⓑ Ⓒ Ⓓ
482. Ⓐ Ⓑ Ⓒ Ⓓ
483. Ⓐ Ⓑ Ⓒ Ⓓ
484. Ⓐ Ⓑ Ⓒ Ⓓ

副詞17

選択肢

(A) initially 副 初めは、当初は (B) abruptly 副 突然に
(C) instantly 副 直ちに (D) utterly 副 全く、完全に

正解・訳

481. (D)

作曲家Davi Morelliによる最近の曲は以前に彼が作曲したものとは<u>全く</u>異なる。

482. (C)

Bisjobs.comは、適した職が雇用主となり得る企業によって掲載されたら<u>直ちに</u>あなたにお知らせします。

483. (A)

操作マニュアルは、<u>当初</u>は英語だけで書かれていたが、現在では10の言語で利用可能である。

484. (B)

そのテレビドラマシリーズは低視聴率のために第2シーズンの始めに<u>突然</u>打ち切られた。

解説

481は空所後の形容詞differentと相性が良い(D) utterly（全く）を選ぶ。completelyも同義語だ。**482**は求人サイトのサービスに関して述べている。良い求人広告が掲載されたら直ちに(instantly)知らせるのが自然。**483**は後半にbut now ...（しかし今では…）とあることから、「今」と対になる(C) initially（当初は）が適切だ。

もう1問！

485. The TV drama series was canceled abruptly at the beginning of its second season due to its low -------.

　　(A) levels (B) rates (C) costs (D) ratings

Unit 9
Set 10

486. The Noble Palms Resort Hotel can now ------- up to 600 guests due to recent expansion.

487. Participants are asked to confirm that their information packets ------- all the necessary documents when they receive them.

488. The manager of the department store approved the installation of a window display to ------- more customers.

489. The public relations department came up with a plan that will ------- customer surveys and more rigorous product testing.

(A) accommodate
(B) contain
(C) attract
(D) involve

問題486~490 Unit 9

486. Ⓐ Ⓑ Ⓒ Ⓓ
487. Ⓐ Ⓑ Ⓒ Ⓓ
488. Ⓐ Ⓑ Ⓒ Ⓓ
489. Ⓐ Ⓑ Ⓒ Ⓓ

選択肢

(A) accommodate 動 ～を収容する　(B) contain 動 ～を含む

(C) attract 動 ～を魅了する　(D) involve 動 ～を含む、～を伴う

正解・訳

486. (A)

最近の拡張によりNoble Palms Resort Hotelはいまや最大600人の宿泊客を収容することが可能となった。

487. (B)

参加者たちは、資料集を受け取り次第、それが必要な書類全てを含んでいることを確認するよう求められている。

488. (C)

デパートの支配人は、より多くの顧客を引き付けるため、ショーウィンドーの設置を承認した。

489. (D)

広報部は顧客アンケートや、さらに厳格な製品テストを含む計画を思い付いた。

come up with ～: ～を思い付く

解説

(A) accommodateは施設などの収容能力を示す際に使う動詞で、**486**のup to 600 guestsのように収容人数を伴って使われることがほとんどだ。(B) containと(D) involveはいずれも「～を含む」という意味を持つが、involveには「関与させる」という意味があり、**489**の文では「計画」に関わる事項を列挙しているイメージだ。

もう1問！

490. The public relations department came up with a plan that will involve customer surveys and more ------- product testing.

(A) remarkable　(B) risky　(C) rigorous　(D) reassured

▶▶▶ 解答は226ページ

Unit 9

Set 11

491. The van was repaired despite its age because buying a new delivery vehicle would be too ------- .

492. Coffee, tea and light snacks are ------- for conference attendees.

493. In online reviews, over 90 percent of customers mentioned our ------- rates.

494. It will be ------- for employees to read the employee manual before the orientation session.

(A) complimentary
(B) beneficial
(C) costly
(D) competitive

問題 491～495　Unit 9

491. Ⓐ Ⓑ Ⓒ Ⓓ
492. Ⓐ Ⓑ Ⓒ Ⓓ
493. Ⓐ Ⓑ Ⓒ Ⓓ
494. Ⓐ Ⓑ Ⓒ Ⓓ

形容詞22

選択肢

(A) complimentary 形 無償の　　(B) beneficial 形 利益がある、役に立つ

(C) costly 形 費用がかかる

(D) competitive 形 (価格などが) 他に負けない、優位性のある

正解・訳

491. (C)

新しい配達用の車両を購入するのはあまりにも費用がかかるため、そのバンは年数が経過していたにも関わらず修理されることとなった。

492. (A)

会議の出席者には、コーヒーや紅茶、軽食が無償で提供される。

493. (D)

オンラインでのレビューでは、90パーセントを超える顧客が、当社の他に負けない価格に言及していた。

494. (B)

導入研修の前に従業員マニュアルを読んでおくことは、従業員にとって有益だろう。

解説

選択肢には価格や利益に関連する形容詞が並んでいる。(C) costly は語尾が ly だが副詞ではなく形容詞なので注意。**492** のように飲み物や軽食が無料 (complimentary) であるという話は TOEIC では鉄板ネタ。(D) competitive は、商品やサービスの価格が他社との競争に負けない、つまり「より安い」ことを表す単語だ。

もう1問！

495. In online reviews, over 90 percent of customers ------- our competitive rates.

(A) demanded　(B) mentioned　(C) surprised　(D) referred

▶▶▶ 解答は226ページ

Unit 9　もう1問！解答一覧

※問題文の訳は(→　)内のページ・番号を参照してください

445. (A)
Although *Commodus* performed very well among young audiences, many film critics thought its script was neither ------- nor sophisticated.

(A) compelling　形 切実な、感動的な　　(B) obsolete　形 廃れた
(C) unbelievable　形 信じられない　　(D) ample　形 十分な

(→ p. 204、**441**)

450. (D)
Ms. Arista was ------- manager of the Madrid branch because of her extensive knowledge of Spanish language and culture.

(A) consulted　動 相談した　　　　　(B) achieved　動 獲得した
(C) proposed　動 提案した　　　　　(D) appointed　動 任命した

(→ p. 206、**446**)

455. (C)
In order to strengthen its relationship with its most ------- client, Steadwell Industries sends representatives to Chicago several times a year.

(A) variable　形 変わりやすい　　　(B) perceptive　形 明敏な
(C) valued　形 大切な　　　　　　(D) premiered　形 初演の、封切られた

(→ p. 208、**453**)

460. (B)
Livida Beauty Products is reportedly in merger talks with an online cosmetics retailer in ------- of expanding its customer base.

(A) cases　名 場合　　　　　　　　(B) hopes　名 希望
(C) terms　名 条件、条項　　　　　(D) charges　名 責任、料金

(→ p. 210、**459**)

465. (D)
Entry to the worksite is prohibited unless you are ------- by a member of the site management team.

(A) anticipated　動 予想された　　　(B) affiliated　動 傘下に置かれた
(C) amended　動 改正された　　　　(D) accompanied　動 同伴された

(→ p. 212、**464**)

もう1問！ Unit 9

470. (C)

In ------- years, there has been a significant increase in the number of foreign workers in Japan.

(A) last 　形 最終の、最新の 　　　(B) multiple 　形 複数の
(C) recent 　形 最近の 　　　　　　(D) numerous 　形 数々の

(→ p. 214、**468**)

475. (D)

The County Health Department will send inspectors to food ------- to confirm their compliance with local regulations.

(A) lines 　　　名 ライン 　　　　(B) expenditures 　名 支出
(C) locations 　名 場所、店舗所在地 　(D) establishments 　名 施設、建物

(→ p. 216、**473**)

480. (C)

By using local -------, the company helps sustain the local economy.

(A) recipients 　名 受信者 　　　(B) participants 　名 参加者
(C) ingredients 　名 材料 　　　　(D) components 　名 要素

(→ p. 218、**479**)

485. (D)

The TV drama series was canceled abruptly at the beginning of its second season due to its low -------.

(A) levles 　名 レベル、段階 　　(B) rates 　名 割合、料金
(C) costs 　名 費用 　　　　　　(D) ratings 　名 視聴率、評価

(→ p. 220、**484**)

490. (C)

The public relations department came up with a plan that will involve customer surveys and more ------- product testing.

(A) remarkable 　形 顕著な 　　(B) risky 　形 危険な
(C) rigorous 　形 厳しい 　　　(D) reassured 　形 安心した

(→ p. 222、**489**)

495. (B)

In online reviews, over 90 percent of customers ------- our competitive rates.

(A) demanded 　動 要求した 　　(B) mentioned 　動 言及した
(C) surprised 　動 驚かせた 　　(D) referred 　動 言及した

(→ p. 224、**493**)

Unit 10
Set 1

496. The company offers ------- to employees who exceed their production targets.

497. Due to a rigorous marketing campaign, sales during the first quarter produced record ------- .

498. The new financial software enables staff to confirm that payments have been made into the company ------- online.

499. On his employee profile, Mr. Carter listed fishing among his ------- .

(A) incentives
(B) profits
(C) accounts
(D) interests

496. Ⓐ Ⓑ Ⓒ Ⓓ
497. Ⓐ Ⓑ Ⓒ Ⓓ
498. Ⓐ Ⓑ Ⓒ Ⓓ
499. Ⓐ Ⓑ Ⓒ Ⓓ

名詞23

選択肢

(A) incentives 名 報奨金　　　　(B) profits 名 利益

(C) accounts 名 口座　　　　　　(D) interests 名 趣味、関心事、利益

正解・訳

496. (A)

その会社は、生産目標を超えた従業員に対して、報奨金を出している。

production target: 生産目標

497. (B)

綿密な販売キャンペーンのおかげで、第1四半期の売上は記録的な利益を生み出した。

rigorous: 綿密な、厳格な

498. (C)

新しい財務ソフトにより、従業員は会社の口座に支払いが行われたことをオンラインで確認することができる。

499. (D)

Carterさんは社員プロフィールに、趣味の1つとして釣りを載せている。

解説

496の(A) incentivesは、生産目標を超えた従業員へ与えられるものとして選ぶことができる。**497**は、販売キャンペーンの成果を伝える内容なので(B) profitsが適切だ。**498**の(C) accountsは銀行やオンラインサービスの「口座」の意味。**499**の(D) interestsは、ここでは「趣味、関心事」の意味だが、「利益」という意味でも頻出する。

もう1問！

500. The company offers incentives to employees who ------- their production targets.

(A) aim　(B) calculate　(C) offset　(D) exceed

▶▶▶ 解答は251ページ

Unit 10
Set 2

501. The board decided to ------- the company's fifth anniversary with a function at the Simpson Conference Hall.

502. In an effort to help ------- the environment, the supermarket urges shoppers to bring their own containers.

503. Customers at GeoMax Online Shopping can ------- points by buying GeoMax brand products and receive discounts on future purchases.

504. Artworks by local painters ------- the walls of the waiting room at Daniels Dental Clinic.

(A) commemorate
(B) decorate
(C) preserve
(D) accumulate

501. Ⓐ Ⓑ Ⓒ Ⓓ
502. Ⓐ Ⓑ Ⓒ Ⓓ
503. Ⓐ Ⓑ Ⓒ Ⓓ
504. Ⓐ Ⓑ Ⓒ Ⓓ

動詞27

選択肢

(A) commemorate 　動　～を祝う　　(B) decorate 　動　～を飾る

(C) preserve 　動　～を保護する　　(D) accumulate 　動　～を集める

正解・訳

501. (A)

理事会は、Simpson Conference Hallにて式典を行い、会社の5周年を祝うことを決定した。

function: 行事、祝典

502. (C)

環境を保護するための努力の一環として、そのスーパーは買い物客に容器を持参するよう促している。

503. (D)

GeoMax Online Shoppingの顧客はGeoMaxブランドの製品を購入することによってポイントを集め、次回以降の購入の際に割引を受けることができる。

504. (B)

地元の画家たちの作品が、Daniels Dental Clinicの待合室を飾っている。

解説

(A)のcommemorateは特別な出来事を祝う際に用いられる。TOEICには企業や自治体が記念日を祝うシーンがよく登場する。環境保護の話題も積極的に取り上げられるので、**502**に入る(C) preserveはenvironment（環境）とともに覚えよう。**504**は主語Artworksや目的語wallsから(B) decorateが正解。

もう1問！

505. In an effort to help preserve the environment, the supermarket ------- shoppers to bring their own containers.

(A) presents　(B) urges　(C) donates　(D) declines

Unit 10
Set 3

506. Social media marketing is very ------- in generating brand awareness and improving customer engagement.

507. The deadline to submit your development project can be extended in ------- circumstances.

508. The sales team was very ------- about the new smartphone models because of the exciting new functions.

509. Orders of over $150 may be ------- for free delivery, depending on their weight.

(A) effective
(B) eligible
(C) exceptional
(D) enthusiastic

506. Ⓐ Ⓑ Ⓒ Ⓓ
507. Ⓐ Ⓑ Ⓒ Ⓓ
508. Ⓐ Ⓑ Ⓒ Ⓓ
509. Ⓐ Ⓑ Ⓒ Ⓓ

形容詞23

選択肢

(A) effective 形 効果的な　　　　(B) eligible 形 資格がある、適格な
(C) exceptional 形 例外の
(D) enthusiastic 形 熱心な、夢中になっている

正解・訳

506. (A)
ソーシャルメディアを利用したマーケティングは、ブランドの認知度を上げ、顧客との関係をより深めることにとても効果的である。
awareness: 認知

507. (C)
開発プロジェクトの提出締め切りは、例外的な状況の場合、延長されうる。
circumstances:（通例、複数形で）状況

508. (D)
販売チームは、そのわくわくするような新機能から、新しいスマートフォンにとても夢中になっている。

509. (B)
150ドルを超える注文をした場合、重さにもよるが、送料無料を適用される。

解説

(A) effectiveは**506**のように前置詞inを伴って「〜に効果がある」という意味になる。同様に**508**の(D) enthusiastic about 〜や**509**の(B) eligible for 〜も、よく一緒に使われる形容詞＋前置詞の組み合わせだ。これらの組み合わせを覚えておくと、選択肢の意味を吟味しなくても解答することができ、時間の節約につながる。

もう1問！

510. Social media marketing is very effective in generating brand awareness and improving customer ------- .

(A) reinforcement (B) township (C) engagement (D) attempt

▶▶▶ 解答は251ページ

Unit 10
Set 4

511. The net profits of Blue Road Industries exceeded the previous year's by a ------- of 13 percent.

512. The furniture for the conference room is in the ------- space on the first floor.

513. The ------- for the upcoming business conference will be announced to the participants via e-mail.

514. Management has decided to close the Sharpton store and send its ------- to the remaining branches.

(A) storage
(B) inventory
(C) venue
(D) margin

511. (A) (B) (C) (D)
512. (A) (B) (C) (D)
513. (A) (B) (C) (D)
514. (A) (B) (C) (D)

問題511~515 Unit 10

233

名詞23

選択肢

(A) storage 名 収納、保管　　(B) inventory 名 在庫

(C) venue 名 開催地　　(D) margin 名 (数量や程度の) 差

正解・訳

511. (D)

Blue Road Industriesの純利益は、前年のそれを13パーセント差で上回った。
net profit: 純利益

512. (A)

会議室で使用する家具は1階の収納スペースにある。

513. (C)

次のビジネス会議の開催地は、参加者にメールで連絡される。

514. (B)

経営者はSharpton店を閉店し、店舗にある在庫を残る店舗に送ることを決定した。

解説

511のby a margin of ~は「~差で」という表現。この言い回しで覚えよう。**512**は、家具を置いておけるのはstorage space (収納スペース)だ。**513**の(C) venueは催し物などが開催される「開催地、会場」のこと。**514**は、閉店した店のものを残る他店に送るという記述から、送るのは(B) inventory (在庫)だと推測できる。

もう1問！

515. Management has decided to close the Sharpton store and send its inventory to the ------- branches.

(A) remaining　(B) encountered　(C) scattering　(D) united

▶▶▶ 解答は251ページ

Unit 10
Set 5

516. We always ------- the processing of corporate orders for auto parts as they usually have a tighter schedule than other customers.

517. The manager ordered the factory to ------- production until a thorough inspection of the assembly line could take place.

518. The advertising campaign failed to ------- sales as much as was hoped.

519. We will refund your money as soon as you ------- a bank account for us to transfer it to.

(A) expedite
(B) halt
(C) boost
(D) designate

516. Ⓐ Ⓑ Ⓒ Ⓓ
517. Ⓐ Ⓑ Ⓒ Ⓓ
518. Ⓐ Ⓑ Ⓒ Ⓓ
519. Ⓐ Ⓑ Ⓒ Ⓓ

選択肢

(A) expedite 動 ～を迅速に処理する、早める　　(B) halt 動 ～を中断させる

(C) boost 動 ～を促進させる　　　　　　　　　(D) designate 動 ～を指定する

正解・訳

516. (A)

法人の日程は他の顧客よりたいてい厳しいため、当社は法人からの自動車部品の注文は常に<u>迅速に処理している</u>。

517. (B)

マネージャーは、組立ラインの徹底的な検査を実施できるまで<u>生産を中断する</u>よう工場に命令した。

518. (C)

その広告キャンペーンは、期待されていたほど<u>売上を促進させる</u>ことができなかった。

519. (D)

送金のための銀行口座を<u>指定して</u>いただき次第、すぐに返金いたします。

解説

516と517は、それぞれ文の後半に記述されている理由がカギとなり、選択肢を絞り込むことができる。516は「日程が厳しい」とあるため(A) expediteが、517は「検査を実施できるまで」とあるため(B) haltが適切だ。519の(D)designateはdesignated area（指定エリア）のように、過去分詞でもよく使われる。

もう1問！

520. The manager ordered the factory to halt production until a -------
inspection of the assembly line could take place.

(A) steep (B) visible (C) clinical (D) thorough

▶▶▶ 解答は251ページ

Unit 10

Set 6

521. Getting to Golden Orb Apartments from the mall is easy, as buses run ------- 10 minutes.

522. Explorer Sports labels ------- of their products with a serial number to verify its authenticity.

523. Because ------- attendees arrived late, the presentation was postponed until 1:00 P.M.

524. Having had so much success at the current address, the store's owner decided to sign ------- 10-year lease.

(A) several
(B) another
(C) each
(D) every

521. Ⓐ Ⓑ Ⓒ Ⓓ
522. Ⓐ Ⓑ Ⓒ Ⓓ
523. Ⓐ Ⓑ Ⓒ Ⓓ
524. Ⓐ Ⓑ Ⓒ Ⓓ

問題521~525　Unit 10

選択肢

(A) several 形 いくつかの   (B) another 形 もう1つの、さらに〜の

(C) each 形 それぞれの   (D) every 形 〜おきの、毎〜

正解・訳

521. (D)

バスが10分おきに運行しているため、ショッピングモールからGolden Orb Apartments へは容易にアクセスできる。

522. (C)

Explorer Sportsは自社製品それぞれに本物であることを証明するためのシリアルナンバーのラベルを貼っている。

523. (A)

何人かの出席者たちの到着が遅れたため、発表は午後1時まで延期された。

524. (B)

店が現在の所在地で大きな成功を収めているので、オーナーはさらに10年の賃貸契約 を結ぶことを決めた。

解説

521の10 minutesと組み合わせられるのは (B) anotherと (D) everyだが、アクセスの便 利さを伝えている文脈では「10分おき」という意味になる(D)が合う。(B)は524の空所 に入り「さらに10年の賃貸契約」という追加を意味する表現となる。(C) eachと (D) everyは意味が近いが、eachは「each of + 名詞の複数形」と表現できるのに対し、every はその使い方はできないことに注意。

もう1問！

525. Explorer Sports ------- each of their products with a serial number to verify its authenticity.

    (A) pastes (B) labels (C) sticks (D) puts

▶▶▶ 解答は252ページ

Unit 10

Set 7

526. To find out the amount you ------- on your gas bill, please contact our customer care department.

527. Tullway Enterprises tends to ------- on Internet advertising rather than print media or television.

528. Maxmore Programming plans to ------- its old computers to a community college after the upgrades are finished.

529. Some freelance writers ------- additional income by providing photographs to go along with their articles.

(A) owe
(B) rely
(C) donate
(D) earn

526. Ⓐ Ⓑ Ⓒ Ⓓ
527. Ⓐ Ⓑ Ⓒ Ⓓ
528. Ⓐ Ⓑ Ⓒ Ⓓ
529. Ⓐ Ⓑ Ⓒ Ⓓ

動詞29

選択肢

(A) owe 動 ～を支払う義務がある　　(B) rely 動 (rely on ～で)～に頼る

(C) donate 動 ～を寄付する　　(D) earn 動 ～を稼ぐ、～を得る

正解・訳

526. (A)

お支払い義務があるガス料金を確認するには、顧客サービス部門にご連絡ください。

527. (B)

Tullway Enterprisesは、活字メディアやテレビよりも、インターネット広告に頼る傾向にある。

tend to: ～する傾向にある

528. (C)

Maxmore Programmingは、保有している古いコンピューターを、アップグレードが完了した後、コミュニティーカレッジに寄付することを計画している。

529. (D)

フリーランスのライターの中には、自分の記事と一緒に掲載する写真を提供することで、追加の収入を得ている者もいる。

解説

空所の直後に前置詞onがある**526**と**527**には自動詞が入り、目的語となる名詞がある**528**と**529**には他動詞が入る。**526**はonの後に支払われるべきものが続いているので(A) oweが適切。**527**の(B) relyはrely on ～ (～に頼る)のセットで覚えよう。depend on ～も同様の意味だ。(D) のearnは「金銭」のほかに「信用」や「名声」なども目的語にできる。

もう1問！

530. Some freelance writers earn additional income by providing photographs to go along with their ------- .

(A) nominations　(B) artifacts　(C) licensees　(D) articles

▶▶▶ 解答は252ページ

Unit 10
Set 8

531. Some schedules on the online calendar are ------- and may change within a few weeks.

532. The company has decided to extend one of its ------- buildings rather than construct a new one.

533. Because the Tailor Public Library was completed to a high standard, Harlequin Constructions was offered further contracts in ------- years.

534. The ------- increase in the cost of fuel has resulted in greater demand for electric cars.

(A) subsequent
(B) tentative
(C) existing
(D) substantial

531. Ⓐ Ⓑ Ⓒ Ⓓ
532. Ⓐ Ⓑ Ⓒ Ⓓ
533. Ⓐ Ⓑ Ⓒ Ⓓ
534. Ⓐ Ⓑ Ⓒ Ⓓ

選択肢

(A) subsequent 形 次の、それに続く　(B) tentative 形 暫定的な
(C) existing 形 既存する　　　　　　(D) substantial 形 かなりの

正解・訳

531. (B)

オンライン上のカレンダーに載っている予定のいくつかは暫定的なもので、数週間以内に変更になる可能性がある。

532. (C)

その会社は新しい建物を建設するよりも、既存の建物のうちの1つを拡張することを決定した。
extend: ～を拡張する

533. (A)

Tailor公立図書館が高い基準で完成したので、Harlequin建設は続く数年間についてさらなる契約の申し出を受けた。

534. (D)

燃料費の大幅な上昇により、電気自動車の需要が大きく高まった。

解説

(A)(B)(C)はいずれも時間や時系列に関する形容詞だ。531は後半で予定変更の可能性を述べているため、予定は(B) tentative (暫定的)だと判断できる。532は新しい建物の建設を否定しているので、(C) existing (既存の)建物を改修する、とすると意味が通る。533は図書館の建設の高評価が、(A) 次の (subsequent) 数年の契約につながったということ。

もう1問！

535. The substantial increase in the cost of fuel has resulted in greater
------- for electric cars.

(A) reduction　(B) demand　(C) availability　(D) attraction

▶▶▶ 解答は252ページ

Unit 10

Set 9

536. Although both graphic designs appear similar, they are ------- different if you examine them closely.

537. I am ------- certain that the president will make a good impression during his introduction speech.

538. Please compile a list of furniture suppliers that ------- offer weekend deliveries.

539. The Katsuma Hotel has a small but ------- equipped fitness center where guests can work out anytime they wish.

(A) specifically
(B) adequately
(C) absolutely
(D) slightly

536. Ⓐ Ⓑ Ⓒ Ⓓ
537. Ⓐ Ⓑ Ⓒ Ⓓ
538. Ⓐ Ⓑ Ⓒ Ⓓ
539. Ⓐ Ⓑ Ⓒ Ⓓ

問題536～540　Unit 10

選択肢

(A) specifically [副] 具体的に言えば、特に　(B) adequately [副] 十分に、適切に

(C) absolutely [副] 完全に、絶対に　(D) slightly [副] わずかに

正解・訳

536. (D)

両方のグラフィックデザインは似ているように見えるが、注意深く見ると<u>わずかに</u>異なっている。

closely: 注意深く

537. (C)

私は、社長が紹介スピーチの間に良い印象を与えることを、<u>完全に</u>確信している。

538. (A)

家具供給会社、<u>具体的に言えば</u>、週末配達サービスを提供している会社のリストを作成してください。

compile: ～（リストなど）を編集する

539. (B)

Katsuma Hotelは、滞在客が望めばいつでも運動できる、小さいが<u>十分に</u>設備がそろったフィットネスセンターを備えている。

解説

537のabsolutely certainは「完全に確信している」＝「非常に強く確信している」という意味。(A)のspecificallyは後に続く節・句を修飾し、より詳細な情報を付加する。**538**では「週末に配達してくれる会社」が知りたいと強調している。**539**では、空所前にあるsmall but（小さいが）とつながり、過去分詞equippedを修飾できる(B)のadequatelyを選ぶ。

もう1問！

540. Although both graphic designs appear similar, they are slightly
------- different if you ------- them closely.

(A) recognize　(B) examine　(C) oversee　(D) depict

▶▶▶ 解答は252ページ

Unit 10
Set 10

541. Competition between streaming video services has
------- , driving down monthly subscription rates.

542. After the two architectural firms merged, the
parking lot was ------- to provide additional spaces
for employees.

543. The hotel has been completely ------- , and it will be
accepting guests from May.

544. Ms. Jones ------- herself with the product manual by
reading it carefully during her flight to New York.

(A) refurbished
(B) familiarized
(C) intensified
(D) enlarged

541. Ⓐ Ⓑ Ⓒ Ⓓ
542. Ⓐ Ⓑ Ⓒ Ⓓ
543. Ⓐ Ⓑ Ⓒ Ⓓ
544. Ⓐ Ⓑ Ⓒ Ⓓ

動詞30

選択肢

(A) refurbished 動 改装した・された

(B) familiarized 動 ～に習熟している・させた

(C) intensified 動 激化した・させた　(D) enlarged 動 ～を拡張した・させた

正解・訳

541. (C)

動画ストリーミングサービスを行っている会社間での競争は激化しており、月額利用料金が引き下げられている。

drive down ~: ～を引き下げる

542. (D)

2つの建築会社が合併した結果、駐車場が拡大され、従業員のためのスペースが追加で提供された。

543. (A)

そのホテルは完全に改装され、5月より宿泊客の受け入れを開始する。

544. (B)

Jonesさんは New York へ向かう飛行機の中で製品マニュアルを丁寧に読み、それに習熟した。

解説

動詞固有の接尾辞や接頭辞を持つ単語は、それらを除いた意味も合わせて覚えよう。(C) の intensify は形容詞 intense (激しい) に「～化する」という意味を添える接尾辞 -fy が付いているので「激化する」という意味だと推測できる。(B) familiarize は familiar (よく知っている) と接尾辞 -ize、(D) enlarge は large (大きい) と接頭辞 en- が組み合わさって動詞化している。

もう1問！

545. After the two architectural firms ------- , the parking lot was enlarged to provide additional spaces for employees.

(A) merged　(B) mixed　(C) combined　(D) completed

▶▶▶ 解答は252ページ

246

Unit 10

Set 11

546. While the interior of the gallery is only ------- complete, it is already being used for exhibitions.

547. Suggestions and complaints from park visitors should be forwarded to the marketing and customer service departments, ------- .

548. An employee survey revealed that wages and career advancement were ------- important.

549. Some of the branches have been generating far more profit than others, ------- Winton, Collingwood and Highcroft.

    (A) equally
    (B) namely
    (C) respectively
    (D) partially

546. Ⓐ Ⓑ Ⓒ Ⓓ
547. Ⓐ Ⓑ Ⓒ Ⓓ
548. Ⓐ Ⓑ Ⓒ Ⓓ
549. Ⓐ Ⓑ Ⓒ Ⓓ

副詞19

選択肢

(A) equally 副 等しく、同様に
(B) namely 副 すなわち、名前は
(C) respectively 副 それぞれ
(D) partially 副 部分的に

正解・訳

546. (D)

画廊の内装は部分的にしか完成していないが、すでに展示に使われている。

547. (C)

公園の来訪者から寄せられた提案と苦情は、それぞれ営業部と顧客サービス部に転送されるべきだ。

548. (A)

従業員意識調査で、賃金と昇進は等しく重要であることが明らかになった。

549. (B)

いくつかの支社は他の支社よりもはるかに大きな利益を上げている。すなわち、Winton、Collingwood、Highcroftの支社である。

解説

547は(C)の副詞respectively（それぞれ）を入れると、「提案は営業部に、苦情は顧客サービスにそれぞれ転送する」という意味になる。文末に置かれることが多い。(B) namelyは、前にある語句を具体的に説明する時に使われ、**549**ではnamelyの後に利益を上げたbranches（支店）の名前を挙げている。

もう1問！

550. Some of the branches have been ------- far more profit than others, namely Winton, Collingwood, and Highcroft.

(A) broadening　(B) striving　(C) offsetting　(D) generating

▶▶▶ 解答は252ページ

Unit 10

Set 12

551. The guide checked that each guest had ------- of water before the tour began.

552. The supervisor thanked ------- the employees for their hard work and contribution in the previous year.

553. As a result of the inclement weather, ------- of the flights from Denver Airport were able to leave on time this morning.

554. Our silk curtain is available as a custom order in ------- of the colors listed in the catalogue.

(A) plenty
(B) none
(C) all
(D) any

551. Ⓐ Ⓑ Ⓒ Ⓓ
552. Ⓐ Ⓑ Ⓒ Ⓓ
553. Ⓐ Ⓑ Ⓒ Ⓓ
554. Ⓐ Ⓑ Ⓒ Ⓓ

代名詞

(A) plenty　代 豊富、多量　　　(B) none　代 どれも～ない
(C) all　代 すべてのもの、人　　(D) any　代 どれも、何も

正解・訳

551. (A)
ガイドはツアーが始まる前に参加客それぞれが<u>十分</u>な水分を補給したか確認した。

552. (C)
上司は、前年の努力と貢献について、従業員<u>全員</u>に感謝した。

553. (B)
悪天候のため、今朝のDenver空港からの飛行機は<u>どれも</u>時間通りに出発<u>できなかった</u>。

554. (D)
当社の絹のカーテンは、カタログに掲載された色の<u>どれでも</u>、特別注文として購入可能です。

解説

(A) plenty は plenty of ~ で「たくさんの～」。可算名詞、不可算名詞どちらも使うことができる。(B) none は、基本的に名詞として使われるので、名詞の前に直接置くことができず、後ろにofが必要。(C) all は「すべてのもの」、(D) any は「どれでも」という意味の代名詞だ。

もう1問！

555. As a result of the ------- weather, none of the flights from Denver Airport were able to leave on time this morning.

　　(A) inclement　(B) infrequent　(C) intuitive　(D) intact

▶▶▶ 解答は253ページ

Unit 10 　もう1問！ 解答一覧

※問題文の訳は(→ 　)内のページ・番号を参照してください

500. (D)
The company offers incentives to employees who ------- their production targets.

(A) aim 　動 〜を狙う　　　　　　(B) calculate 　動 〜を計算する
(C) offset 　動 〜を相殺する　　　　(D) exceed 　動 〜を上回る
(→ p. 228、496)

505. (B)
In an effort to help preserve the environment, the supermarket ------- shoppers to bring their own containers.

(A) presents 　動 〜を見せる　　　　(B) urges 　動 〜を促す
(C) donates 　動 〜を寄付する　　　　(D) declines 　動 〜を断る
(→ p. 230、502)

510. (C)
Social media marketing is very effective in generating brand awareness and improving customer ------- .

(A) reinforcement 　名 強化　　　　　(B) inquiry 　名 問い合わせ
(C) engagement 　名 関与、エンゲージメント (D) attempt 　名 試み
(→ p. 232、506)

515. (A)
Management has decided to close the Sharpton store and send its inventory to the ------- branches.

(A) remaining 　形 残りの　　　　　(B) encountered 　形 遭遇した
(C) scattering 　形 分散した　　　　(D) united 　形 団結した
(→ p. 234、514)

520. (D)
The manager ordered the factory to halt production until a ------- inspection of the assembly line could take place.

(A) steep 　形 急勾配の　　　　　　(B) visible 　形 目に見える
(C) clinical 　形 臨床の　　　　　　(D) thorough 　形 徹底的な、綿密な
(→ p. 236、517)

もう1問！ Unit 10

525. (B)

Explorer Sports ------- each of their products with a serial number to verify its authenticity.

(A) pastes 動 張り付ける
(B) labels 動 ラベルを貼る
(C) sticks 動 刺す、（ピンなどで）留める
(D) puts 動 付ける

(→ p. 238、**522**)

530. (D)

Some freelance writers earn additional income by providing photographs to go along with their ------- .

(A) nominations 名 指名
(B) artifacts 名 人工物、芸術品
(C) licensees 名 被許諾者、ライセンシー
(D) articles 名 記事

(→ p. 240、**529**)

535. (B)

The substantial increase in the cost of fuel has resulted in greater ------- for electric cars.

(A) reduction 名 削減
(B) demand 名 需要、要求
(C) availability 名 利用可能性
(D) attraction 名 魅力、呼び物

(→ p. 242、**534**)

540. (B)

Although both graphic designs appear similar, they are slightly different if you ------- them closely.

(A) recognize 動 ～を認める
(B) examine 動 ～を詳細に見る
(C) oversee 動 ～を監視する
(D) depict 動 ～を描く

(→ p. 244、**536**)

545. (A)

After the two architectural firms ------- , the parking lot was enlarged to provide additional spaces for employees.

(A) merged 動 合併した
(B) mixed 動 ～を混ぜた
(C) combined 動 ～を合成した
(D) completed 動 ～を完了した

(→ p. 246、**542**)

550. (D)

Some of the branches have been ------- far more profit than others, namely Winton, Collingwood and Highcroft.

(A) broadening 動 ～を拡大している
(B) striving 動 努力している
(C) offsetting 動 ～を相殺している
(D) generating 動 ～を生み出している

(→ p. 248、**549**)

555. (A)

As a result of the ------- weather, none of the flights from Denver Airport were able to leave on time this morning.

(A) inclement 形 荒れ模様の
(B) infrequent 形 まれな
(C) intuitive 形 直感的な
(D) intact 形 無傷の、完全なままの

(→ p. 250、**553**)

アルクは個人、企業、学校に
語学教育の総合サービスを提供しています。

英 語

通信講座

1000 HOUR **HEARING MARATHON**　　**TOEIC®対策**

『イングリッシュ・クイックマスター』シリーズ

ほか

書 籍

キクタン　ユメタン

『起きてから寝るまで』シリーズ

TOEIC® ／ TOEFL® ／ 英検®

ほか

月刊誌

ENGLISH JOURNAL

辞書データ検索サービス

英辞郎 on the WEB Pro

オンライン会話

アルク オンライン 英会話

アプリ

『キクタン』シリーズ

ほか

セミナー

TOEIC®対策 セミナー

ほか

子ども英語教室

アルク Kiddy CAT 英語教室

留学支援

アルク 留学センター

学 校

eラーニング

ALC NetAcademy NEXT

学習アドバイス

ESAC

書 籍

高校・大学向け 副教材

企 業

団体向けレッスン

クリエイティブ スピーキング

ほか

スピーキングテスト

TSST

TOEIC® L&Rテスト
Part 5
語彙問題だけ555

発行日：2020年4月20日（初版）

監修：西嶋愉一

著者：勝山庸子、小林佳奈子、下窄称美、山田 治

編集：株式会社アルク出版編集部

校正：Peter Branscombe、Margaret Stalker、Ross Tulloch

カバーデザイン：トサカデザイン（戸倉 巌、小酒保子）

本文デザイン・DTP：朝日メディアインターナショナル株式会社

ナレーション：Chris Koprowski、菊地信子、岡本 昇

印刷・製本：萩原印刷株式会社

発行者：田中伸明

発行所：株式会社アルク

〒102-0073　東京都千代田区九段北 4-2-6 市ヶ谷ビル
Website: https://www.alc.co.jp/

地球人ネットワークを創る

アルクのシンボル
「地球人マーク」です。